THE PARALLAX FROM HELL

Satan's Critique of Organized Religion and Other Essays

Douglas L. Laubach

iUniverse, Inc.
Bloomington

The Parallax from Hell
Satan's Critique of Organized Religion and Other Essays

iUniverse books may be ordered through booksellers or by contacting:

iUniverse
1663 Liberty Drive
Bloomington, IN 47403
www.iuniverse.com
1-800-Authors (1-800-288-4677)

Because of the dynamic nature of the Internet, any web addresses or links contained in this book may have changed since publication and may no longer be valid. The views expressed in this work are solely those of the author and do not necessarily reflect the views of the publisher, and the publisher hereby disclaims any responsibility for them.

Any people depicted in stock imagery provided by Thinkstock are models, and such images are being used for illustrative purposes only.

Certain stock imagery © Thinkstock.

ISBN: 978-1-4697-9835-6 (sc)
ISBN: 978-1-4697-9833-2 (e)
ISBN: 978-1-4697-9834-9 (dj)

Library of Congress Control Number: 2012904949

Printed in the United States of America

iUniverse rev. date: 4/25/2012

Do not believe in anything simply because you have heard it. Do not believe in anything simply because it is spoken and rumoured by many. Do not believe in anything simply because it is found written in your religious books. Do not believe in anything merely on the authority of your teachers and elders. Do not believe in traditions because they have been handed down for many generations. But after observation and analysis, when you find that anything agrees with reason and is conducive to the good and benefit of one and all, then accept it and live up to it.

—Buddha

Contents

Book II Satan's Soliloquy

Introduction

I have found you an argument; I am not obliged to find you an understanding.
—Dr. Samuel Johnson

Whenever one wishes to learn of a religion and picks up a book that gives a general outline of each of the major religions, one will find the authors apparently feel duty bound to affirm to their readership that all the major religions have common bonds (they believe in one God, the Golden Rule, etc.), have traditions of serving the spiritual needs of mankind, and that they all seem to coexist in a world that has multifaceted spiritual wants and needs. In short, the authors write as if to imply that all religions serve a noble purpose, so as not to cast a shadow over their illustrious images. Seldom will an author who is covering more than one religion in his or her work bring out the less than desirable traits of the religions being examined. They fail with purpose to cover obscure but significant details that demonstrate the baser beliefs of those religions. I wish to correct that wrong.

Many people know little of the basic tenants and history of their own faiths and much less of the faith of others. Religion, to the majority, is more of a tradition than it is a way of life and personal creed. People belong to their churches, synagogues, mosques, or temples usually because, like their parents before them, as children they attended services with their family and developed a comfort level with their family's religion. It is the "faith of our fathers" syndrome. The fraternal activities of the membership and the subsequent community ties that are thus created develop a strong bond among the members of the congregation, which reinforces the member's tendency to remain within the religion of his childhood.

Obviously this is a generalization, and there are numerous people who change or lose their religions for various reasons. The major religions, however, tend to perpetuate themselves by becoming an integral part of family life or of the community. They do this by encouraging attendance to worship services; conducting special projects; providing child care; sanctioning marriages, baptisms, funerals; and participating in a host of other activities that tie the individual to the religious community. Some people are so reliant upon their church, temple, synagogue, or mosque that they become totally submissive to its discipline.

The church, synagogue, temple, or mosque as a community institution obviously fills several needs. The concept of a local benevolent body of people congregating together in fellowship is the image that most people have of their own religions. Unfortunately, hidden behind this benign portrait of beneficence is a hidden agenda and a mass of doctrine that is often contradictory to the vision members have of their own church.

The average congregation of any religious institution is unschooled in church doctrine. Or, if indoctrinated through catechisms or other instruction, the member receives biased and one-sided information that is based on the religion's interpretation of its holy books and other ecclesiastical sources. True believers are not introspective.

For example, Catholics are taught the doctrine of papal infallibility. The pope speaks for God and is never wrong. They don't discuss the times various popes have made declarations only to have such declarations countermanded by a successor.

The Catholic Church, through its pope, once declared the earth to be flat and only recently recanted. Papal infallibility is a false doctrine built upon the power of persuasion of the church over its true believers.

Mormons are taught that Joseph Smith came upon ancient gold plates and interpreted those plates into the English version of the Book of Mormon. The Mormons have developed an impressive bureaucracy, educational system, and missionary program. They educate their members and help formulate strong family ties to the church. Yet how many Mormons have studied the origins of their religion with any degree of objectivity? How many of them are aware that Joseph Smith, their prophet, copied most of the Book of Mormon ("inspired" in 1828, first published in 1830) from contemporary sources such as Ethan Smith's (no relationship) book entitled *View of the Hebrews* (published in 1825)? A considerable portion of the Book of Mormon reads verbatim from the King James Version of the Old Testament. Any objective researcher can come to the obvious and correct conclusion about how the Book of Mormon originated from a wealth of primary source material easily available at the time of its authorship.

How many Muslims know or even care that their Prophet, who claimed to receive divine inspiration from God, frequently had "revelations" that became suras of the Koran, which were in fact special licenses for Mohammad to take actions that were contradictory to his earlier teachings during his ministry at Mecca? Well respected, successful, and powerful in Medina, he had revelations contradicting his earlier messages. These "revelations" justified his actions when he sought to take more than one wife, to promote intolerance of other religions and kill nonbelievers who opposed his rule, to justify raids on caravans for profit, to settle old scores by assassinating political opposition, to justify the massacre of the Banu Qurayza Jews at Medina and his theft of their property, and to pursue other such self-serving "revelations" that were then viewed as God's permission for Mohammed to indulge in unsavory and immoral endeavors.

The issue I raise is that theological studies by religious participants tend to be less than objective and, for the most part, self-serving. They practice selective omission of documented facts when it serves their purposes. They turn a blind eye to controversial issues lest they unravel the whole ecclesiastical edifice. While cleric and scholars have knowledge or access to much of the obscure history and theology, they hide the facts from their membership, ignore the facts, or, if necessary, defend and act as apologists for the shortcomings of their doctrine. *These religious scholars are, in reality, defenders of the faith.* They pretend to practice an objective, scholarly approach to religious studies, but their religious bias does not allow them to coldly dissect and criticize a doctrine in which they have a vested interest and an emotional attachment. They make subtle differentiations between historical truth, religious truth, and symbolic truth, and then they confuse the uninformed with their sophistry.

Unlike the clerics and theologians, most lay people who profess to a certain faith are simply ignorant of challenges to church doctrine, unaware of factual or theological contradictions, and have no knowledge of the history of their religion other than what they may have been taught by their own church fathers. The faithful believe what they are told and attend church regularly; the marginal members ignore whatever issues they deem to be unacceptable and still attend services with some degree of regularity.

Faith of our fathers perpetuates itself. Docile, unengaged members continue to practice their religion in the tradition of their fathers. They are going through the motions assuming it will provide their children with the foundations for a moral adult life as measured by the doctrines of whatever religion to which they subscribe. "If it was good enough for my parents and their parents, it is good enough for my family and me."

Examining the validity of one's personal religious foundations is left to those few individuals who have an interest in close, objective evaluation of the religious doctrines with which they and their progeny would be associated. These are rare individuals, indeed, who take the time to critically and objectively study the doctrines of their faith.

Surely any religion that constitutes one's core beliefs and one's framework of morality deserves more circumspection than succumbing to Paul the apostle's exhortations to "become fools so that you may become wise." "For the wisdom of this world is foolishness with God ..." (1 Cor. 3:19, KJV). Why would any person willingly become a slave to a belief that requires unquestioning faith? Why does a religion discourage questions about its theology unless it has something to fear from scrutiny?

Most people are more careful with their jobs, businesses, or their possessions than they are with their immortal souls. Could it be that when it comes to religious doctrine, they just don't *really* believe? For many, a religion is nothing more than a means of achieving social respectability and acceptance into the community. For some it is simply insurance against the possibility that salvation of the soul is a valid concept.

Or could it be that they believe what they have been taught to believe, trusting that the theologians professing to have the answers really know what they are talking about? Is it really a sin not to accept the theological teachings of anyone without a dose of healthy skepticism? I submit that if a person truly, truly believes in an afterlife, that person should make an effort to come to terms with God on an independently researched and informed understanding of the concepts surrounding belief in a Supreme Being.

A religious belief should be founded on solid principals and certain universal truths. If those "truths" are suspect, incomprehensible, or contradictory, keep looking. The world is full of religions, all competing for your soul. Some want to save you from Hell; others have different objectives. Make them show you they are worthy of becoming custodians of your soul. Convince yourself that they can keep the promises they make to their true believers. Learn their history, their dirty laundry, how they are structured, and especially the doctrine they teach and how their teachings may differ from the writings of their holy books. Spend some time learning what others say and write about your favorite religion. And don't feel guilty if you have doubts. Religious tyranny is a device used to keep the flock faithful and docile. It is only effective when you allow it to be used against you to make you fearful or guilty. Who was it that said, "And ye shall know the truth and the truth shall set you free"?

Faith without some element of factual support is a poor foundation on which to base one's personal creed of living. A religion based primarily on faith is detrimental to the spiritual and moral growth of the individual. Such religions and cults cannot afford to tolerate logical inquiry into the very foundations of their existence. Thus a canon is devised, and the prime directive to its members is to have faith and believe. Those who do not agree with the canon or show a lack of faith are branded apostates, heretics or pagans. A religion founded solely on faith or myth becomes intolerant of other beliefs. It becomes paranoid in the defense of its founding principles and must be on constant guard against heresy, defending whatever person, myth, book, or event upon which it bases its faith.

A certain amount of faith is required in all day-to-day activities. If a man is hired to build a house, one should not take it on faith that he knows his trade; references should be required and verified. The only element one might leave to faith (chance?) is whether or not the builder can undertake and finish the task within the terms agreed upon. But that small act of faith is supported by the fact that the builder has previously completed dozens of similar projects without loss or complaint by his clients. Thus this act of faith is supported by critical evidence that allows one to make a reasonably informed decision.

A sound religious doctrine should invite and be able to withstand inquiry and criticism by its own members. It should encourage its members to seek out whatever truths they can glean from the immense volumes written on religions, philosophy, and morality. No religion or creed should shackle its members by making them feel guilty or ostracized while they search for spiritual peace and harmony. Such religions serve as locks and chains to the soul. Any religion founded on the beguiling premise that the believer need only have faith and believe unequivocally in whatever canon the priests and elders have devised for the membership is guilty of suborning the minds and spirits of its members. Just as some degree of faith in one's fellow man is required to conduct the affairs of daily living, so is a certain amount of faith necessary to any creed, doctrine, or religion. But when a monumental leap of faith is required, the essence of one's being should not be the stakes.

Do you believe and have faith in your chosen religion as the result of independent thinking and a bit of research, or do you "believe" because the thinking has already been done for you and you feel safe in the company of *true believers*? And, if you are an atheist or nonbeliever, don't be smug; does your own creed or religion rest on any firmer ground?

The Threefold Mystical Path, the Eightfold Path, the Divine Path, the Way, the Spiritual Path, and all other Paths of Illumination are simply different and well-meaning routes within the same universal labyrinth from which there is no escape.

—Satan

Prologue

*An apology for the devil: It must be remembered
that we have heard only one side of the case. God
has written all the books.*

—Samuel Butler

My name is Satan. Some call me Lucifer; others have called
me such names as Ball, Baal, Mephistopheles, Berith, Iblis,
Abaddon, Beelzebub, or other such names of ancient gods in
decline. Some people say I was created by God (YHWH) and
given power over humankind as the result of the original sin
committed by Adam and Eve. Others maintain that I, Satan, am
actually the God of the Old Testament. It has also been argued
that I am not real but am merely the concept of evil. And, of
course, many simply believe I do not even exist.

The Hebrew word, Satan, is derived from a root word
meaning "oppose," or "accuse."[1] Even the first books of the Bible
refer to the word *satan* as a common noun, and not necessarily a
proper noun. A *satan* is one who opposes or accuses. I suppose
by this definition, the inquisitors, papists, and their supporters
who took part in the persecutions and inquisitions associated
with the Holy Catholic Church could be labeled as such, but it
seems contradictory to call such reverent men *satans*. Or does it?

---

1 Russell, *Satan: The Early Christian Tradition*, 27.

Unfortunately, it is the way of men that the politically weaker or losing side of such holy feuds is usually the group that is declared in league with Satan. The losers are the heretics, and the winners are the ardent "defenders of the faith." History is never written by the losers.

You may find my manner objectionable and opinions acrimonious, but any factual information or references to facts or events will be substantiated, referenced, and even footnoted where deemed necessary. It would be regrettable should any reader dismiss any unpleasant fact or truth as a lie. If I fail to footnote any statement of fact, rest assured that you can find it documented in the bibliography of this book. Nothing stated as fact or history set down on these pages has been written without an independent source of reference. So if you find a statement of fact objectionable, do your own research. My opinions, of course, are the result of a long list of experiences with the human race and its egocentric nature. Such opinions are born of firsthand experience, need no defense, and stand on their own merits. Give the Devil his due.

What you read may be the work of the Devil, but it will be factual and verifiable. I would venture to say what you find in this text is truth—but as is beauty, truth is in the eye of the beholder. Those who object to this work will have to twist the truth and facts presented to fit their own interpretations and dogma. And when one makes the statement (as some will surely do when confronted with facts that are contrary to dogma), "But things are different now," know that mankind has not changed a bit from the dawn of recorded history. He is motivated today by the same traits that inspired and provoked him when he lived in caves. He is just better educated and more sophisticated at masking those traits today.

You should not judge harshly the poor, unfortunate soul I chose to pen this manuscript. He went in search of the Truth and he found me, instead. Since no one wishes to be my advocate, I have elected to defend myself through this modern-day paladin. Ironically, as he writes this he still does not really believe I'm using him. He thinks he's involved in an exercise of philosophical iconoclasm. Yet without my input, his whole effort would be nothing but mental masturbation. Thomas Aquinas he is not. Burn the heretic if you wish. After all, if you are reading this, he has served my purpose and I am finished with him. God's will and your revenge upon him will only vindicate me and prove the point of this entire endeavor. You will have proven my claim that God created both good and evil and that Satan (yours truly, if I exist at all) does not create nor spawn the evil that men do. The ultimate responsibility for the existence of evil belongs with God. And man himself, not I, is responsible for the evil that men do. I repeat, *man* is responsible for the evil in this world; yet that institution known as the church continues to shift blame from mankind to me, Satan.

The infliction of cruelty with a good conscience is a delight to moralists—that is why they invented hell.

—Bertrand Russell

BOOK I
THE DEVIL'S ADVOCATE

Truth is not a creed, but a light which illuminates all creeds.

—Myrtle Reed (1874–1911)

The Mythmakers

Mythology is what grown-ups believe, folklore is what they tell children, and religion is both.
—Cederic Whitman

This book was written as a means to encourage the reader to examine his or her beliefs without relying on dogma or blind faith. Christ is quoted as saying that you must be converted and become as little children if you are to enter the kingdom of Heaven (Matt. 18:3, KJV). A child believes what he is told by his parents without question. As the child grows older, he realizes that he must question certain things that he had been led to believe as the unquestioned truth. Often he discovers that what parents, teachers, or even friends want him to accept is their version of the truth, with certain facts omitted for his own good.

It is unfortunate, but a child loses his innocence when he gains knowledge. Just as little Johnny discovers there really is no Santa Claus or Easter Bunny, so must a man learn to question and examine those things that he has been told since birth are unalterable truths.

Slowly truths turn into half-truths, which ultimately turn into lies. "Well, Johnny, you are right; there really is no Santa Claus as you understood. But, Johnny, there is the spirit of Christmas, which is the same as the spirit of Santa Claus. So long as you believe there is a spirit of Christmas and Santa, then, yes, Santa does exist."

Of course no one tells little Johnny that Santa is a pagan symbol that Christianity has adopted over time or that the concept of the Easter egg stems from the Gnostics and was copied from the lore of the Orphicists.[2] These are the half-truths he can only discover by continuing to question what he is told by those he should have been able to trust.

When a person is truly "converted," he has total faith in the belief into which he was converted. He is complete and at peace with himself. And when a person has complete and total faith in an idea or belief, his mind closes to any further debate or examination of the subject. If he "knows" in his heart that he is right, why should he subject himself and his belief to criticism or possible iconoclasm? Any new knowledge becomes extraneous clutter that might confuse or place a seed of doubt in the convert's mind. And since lack of faith is a cardinal sin to the true believer, partaking of the Tree of Knowledge puts one's soul in jeopardy.

New information or knowledge would simply destroy the newfound peace of the convert. Who wants to chance the discovery that his basic creed in life is founded upon deception, myth, and lies? By eating from the Tree of Knowledge, Adam and Eve lost their innocence and were cast out of Eden. Who needs such grief? For the true believer, ignorance is truly bliss.

> *The habit of religion is oppressive, an easy way out of thought.*
> —Peter Ustinov

---

2 Robertson, *Pagan Christs*, 53.

Fallen Angel, Tool of God, or Superstition?

*The Christians were the first to make the existence
of Satan a dogma of the church.*
— Madame Elena Blavatsky

Most religions are cults that begin with a prophet proclaiming that the new religion is the Truth and the Way. Later, when the followers have become more organized and have found their place among the surviving religions of the time, they shift the focus of their zeal. First they must protect souls from false religions. Then they must protect those same souls from heresies within their own organization. And, once those goals are more or less accomplished, the religious organization must protect the true believer from the clutches of Satan. That's where I come into the picture.

You see, if I did not exist, I would have to be created by someone. One of the warrior religions, Christianity, is literally based on my existence. I am the antagonist to the protagonist, Christ. I am the reason for Armageddon. From the church's viewpoint, I am Christ's reason for being.

In all candor, none of the religions on Earth can agree on just who or what I am. Each religion has its own version of the "truth" based on hearsay (revelation) or "gospels" written and rewritten by self-serving people with their own agendas for the minds of men.

How can these religions each profess to condemn me when they cannot even agree on my name, the level of my culpability, my ultimate guilt in the (alleged) fall of man, or even my very existence? Should you take the time to read the Bible, Koran, Bhagavad Gita, Book of Mormon, Urantia Book, the Torah, the Kabbalah, and other "holy" books, you will realize that the paths to the "Truth and the Way" (a.k.a. salvation) are as numerous as there are religious sects and philosophies. These "Words of God" frequently contradict each other and even accuse other holy books and writings of falsehoods, blasphemy, and error. So much for the "infallible word of God" as set down by mankind.

The testaments against me are all different and without confirmed authorship. I have been condemned and convicted without benefit of the proper facts being presented in my defense. There is not even agreement among Christians as to my relationship with God and Christ. Did God send Christ to Earth as a ransom or as a sacrifice to me in exchange for the souls of man? Why would an omnipotent God barter with a lesser being such as me? If Christ is God, and God is omnipotent, then how could I be responsible for any of Christ's problems or persecution here on Earth? If an omnipotent God created me, what is my reason for existing?

A Manifesto

Religion is an illusion and it derives its strength from the fact that it falls in with our instinctual desires.

—Sigmund Freud

It is with the institution of organized religion I take issue and pen my advocacy. I proclaim my innocence of the sins of men and refusal to take responsibility for the damnation of their souls. It is the true believer and his religious institution that creates and interprets myths and laws, which are used against his fellow man. I neither create these laws nor enforce the punishments against those who transgress the laws of God as set forth by mere mortals on Earth.

Furthermore, I maintain that more earthly death and destruction has been thrust upon mankind by organized religion than by Satan or whomever you wish to call me. Religious wars continue to rage around the world, but all participants are "defenders of the faith" worshiping God, not me. Likewise, I have never damned a soul to Hell, but many a clergy has done so. Remember, also, that the evil perpetrated in God's name by those who would save the souls of mankind was created not by me, but by omnipotent God. Why, then, am I the one being associated with bad and evil while all religions are associated with good and godliness? (Obviously, my public relations director is a total incompetent.)

If you strongly believe in the existence of the devil, then you have probably already drawn your own conclusion; you know that Satan has corrupted the author of this work or at the very least has manifested his evil through these pages. Being a devout believer, you will condemn this book to Hell from whence it came and not chance reading the contents. After all, any reader of Genesis knows that knowledge is associated with Satan. It is the forbidden fruit from which poor Adam ate. I am the angel of light, of knowledge, and for that I have been cursed by the warrior religions that seek to keep their believers well protected from knowledge (heresy?) with a cloak of ignorance.

The true believer who has genuine fear of God and absolute faith in the Bible or Koran will not be influenced by the words I write. But standing on the shifting sands of pious principle, he or she may choose not to read the words within this tome. In my experience, the God-fearing believer will hold the position that anyone attempting to provide facts, knowledge, or opinion contrary to the true faith is trying to corrupt the eternal soul. He or she will flatly state that such writings as this do the devil's work, and one would be advised to read no further. They might even suggest that by avoiding the pages of this book the reader will have avoided becoming one of Satan's unwitting tools. And thus, having eluded my web of forbidden knowledge, you, dear reader, will possibly have saved your soul from Hell. Now, I submit that reading this work isn't so serious an offense to the church or to God as to send anyone to Hell. If you already have a reservation for Hell, reading this book will not change your destiny. Still, while you may not save your soul from Hell, you may indeed save yourself from religious or political ideologies, popular opinion, myth, the "truth," or even from yourself. One must wonder: Is it better to be saved from an uncertain Hell or from those in the real temporal world who would enslave your mind and control your beliefs?

If you are agnostic—that is, if you believe that *maybe* there is a Satan and/or a God, but you aren't certain—then perhaps you will view this work as an opportunity to make your own informed decision as to my relationship with God and with mankind. At least you should be willing to read it objectively before you condemn me or burn this book.

For my purposes, it matters not what you currently believe or disbelieve. Belief, by definition, is not the same as fact and is definitely not synonymous with the truth. My goal is to set the record straight concerning what organized religion is teaching about me. I am not proselyting recruits for any cause or religion. I simply wish to force mankind and his religious institutions to take personal responsibility for thoughts and actions and quit blaming me when rationalization fails them.

If you believe that I am the nemesis of mankind, then you already know my reputation for temptation, corruption, and hate. It is an unjust reputation, and I shall attempt to clear my name. If you don't believe I exist, know then that there have been very evil doings in this world, and while they have all been laid at my hooves, I am not to blame for the wickedness in this world. Evil is God's creation, not mine. Like Job, Christ, Mohammed, Moses, Judas Iscariot, and others, I am merely a suffering servant doing God's will.

Terrible things continue to happen on this world. Wars rage, terrorism runs amuck, disease plagues us, and at times nature shakes off mankind like a dog shakes off fleas. To pious victims, such awful catastrophes are viewed as a test of faith, much like the tests God suffered upon His loyal servant Job. Personal tragedy is simply God's will. But should the same fate befall apostates and infidels, such affliction is considered God's scourge upon their heresy; they are suffering God's wrath. *Yet is there really any difference between God's will for His chosen and His wrath for the wicked?*

I submit that the source of all pain, suffering, and misery on Earth is caused not from Satan, but from God. I may be responsible for tormenting lost souls in Hell, but God is omnipotent and rules over all, even my beloved Hell. God signs my paycheck!

So join me now as we explore the perimeters of Heaven and Hell. As I allegedly gave the "forbidden" fruit of knowledge to Adam and Eve, I am now about to do the same for you. I just hope you do a better job of using the information than they did.

> *Religion is the source of all imaginable follies and disturbances; it is the parent of fanaticism and civil discord; it is the enemy of mankind.*
> —Voltaire

The Dogma of Organized Religions

A religion can no more afford to degrade its Devil than to degrade its God.

—Havelock Ellis

Milton, in *Paradise Lost*, cast me as the errant angel who waged war upon God in Heaven and caused man to be cast out from Paradise. Dante was more allegorical in his approach to Hell and salvation when he wrote the *Divine Comedy*. My favorite version of the myth is Steven Brust's tale of the revolt in Heaven in his novel *To Reign in Hell*. Brust at least recognized that I have no need to lie when I try to explain my opposition to Yawah's Great Plan. He also did a better job of demonstrating how poorly I handled the events that led to my need to take leave of Heaven. I never mastered the art of the lie.

And, of course, Goethe's *Faust* can be blamed for wrongly promoting the idea that I deal in men's souls. Marlow wrote *Doctor Faustus*, one of several tellings of the Faust legend. Goethe's version ends with Faust being saved from my clutches by a band of angels who take him to Heaven. Marlowe's version has Faustus being dragged down to Hell in payment for selling his soul to the devil. I take exception to the medieval tales that disparage my reputation. Souls belong to God. He created them, and they are His property; He does with them as He sees fit. I may be a fallen angel, but I am no thief. I have no need to steal from God and incur His anger.

Of course, if I made God angry with me, he wouldn't cast me out and send me to Hell; God did that some time ago when none of His other archangels wanted the position of adversary to man. It is a dirty job, but someone had to do it and God chose me. And following God's example, Christ chose Judas Iscariot to bear the eternal damnation of being labeled a betrayer so He could fulfill a Jewish prophecy and lay claim to the title of Messiah. As much as it will disgust you to know, dear true believer, God and I have a special arrangement. He created me and He cast me out to play a part in this cosmic play. If God were truly angry with me He could simply have me cease to exist as easily as when (if?) He created me.

Hebrews 2:14 of the Christian New Testament states that Jesus Christ sought to destroy me through His death. He died, yet here I am, still playing the part of the bogeyman for Christians, Muslims, and Jews. So, tell me again, please, just why Christ was crucified?

> *Dogma does not mean the absence of thought,*
> *but the end of thought.*
> —Gilbert Keith Chesterton

The Original Sin, Revisited

Theology is an attempt to explain a subject by men who do not understand it. The intent is not to tell the truth but to satisfy the questioner.

—Elbert Hubbard

Actually (and in spite of what Hebrews 2:14 says), Christian dogma declares that Christ was crucified to save you all from the original sin of Adam and Eve. The "sin" that has damned the entire human species from the Christian point of view is that of Adam and Eve disobeying God's commandment that they should not eat the fruit of the tree in the Garden of Eden. (The Jews didn't take it quite so hard and just marked it up to one of many mistakes that God's chosen have made in their long-term relationship with YHWH.)

According to the Book of Genesis, God promised Adam and Eve death if they ate the fruit of the tree; I promised them only that they would learn to tell the difference between good and evil, "For God doth know that in the day ye eat thereof, then your eyes shall be opened, and ye shall be as gods, knowing good and evil" (Gen. 3:5, KJV). Is that so wrong?

My own promise to Adam and Eve was kept. They did learn the difference between good and evil. *Isn't that what God wants of His children—to know the difference between good and evil?*

That is certainly what the church maintains is part of its mission. So why am I the bad guy here?

In Genesis 3:3 (KJV), He says to Adam and Eve, " But of the fruit of the tree which is in the midst of the garden, God hath said, Ye shall not eat of it, neither shall ye touch it, lest ye die." But they did not die because, luckily for them, God didn't fulfill His earlier threat. Nor did God punish Eve with much more than pain in childbearing for women and Adam with a lifetime of toiling in the fields for food. Of course, in Genesis the Bible tells us that God originally put Adam in the Garden of Eden to till it and keep it, so Adam's punishment wasn't much more than a slap on the wrist. He just had to go elsewhere to till the soil.

In spite of what Christianity teaches about God's punishment of man for Adam and Eve's transgression, He did not cast them out from the Garden of Eden because they defied Him; He cast them out because of His fear that Adam would next eat from the tree of life and become immortal! Genesis 3:22–24 (KJV) relates the passage very plainly. He even placed a cherubim and flaming sword at the east of the garden to guard the way to the tree of life. I'm surprised some intrepid explorer hasn't yet stumbled upon this amazing sight.

> *It is to be believed because it is absurd.*
> —Quintus Septimus Tertullianus
> (Christian Apologist)

Dogma Does Not Equal Truth

Priests are no more necessary to religion than politicians to patriotism.

—John H. Holmes

My point in this section is that organized religion has created and fostered its own interpretations of its holy books, especially the Bible, the Torah, and the Koran. If read independently without outside influence, a completely different understanding of these books and the religion they profess to support can be established by a reader who has not been exposed to the precepts of Christianity, Judaism, and Islam. The same would go for any other such religious tome.

An independent understanding of God's Word can lead to hard questions that cannot be answered by religious theologians. More to the point, *an independent understanding of the Bible or other holy books can lead to heresies.* Religions don't like heretics because heretics undermine the "true faith," which is the foundation upon which organized religion is built. Heretics create schisms within an organization that threaten to reduce the power of the defenders of the faith. If one piece of dogma can be successfully challenged, then another might be called into question. Before long the entire fabric begins to unravel. I contend that the self-appointed defenders of the faith are not policing the "Word of God," rather they are defending their own claim to power and position through absolute control and interpretation of the religion's creed. Hence, the real problem with heresy is that heretics pose a direct threat to the organization and its priestly power structure, not to the creed itself.

And if you doubt the truth of this claim, consider the fact that all religions have gradually evolved and subtly revised and changed their canon over time and as conditions warrant. Yet, when these same changes were first proposed by members within the sect contrary to the wishes of the dominant priesthood, the members were called heretics and blasphemers.

Rather than recount any one of hundreds of such stories in detail, check out a copy of Foxe's *Book of Martyrs* and read a few of the examples of Christian intolerance for dissensions, such as the history and martyrdom of Bishop Ridley and Bishop Latimer, who were both burned at the stake by their fellow Christians for disagreeing over several issues of church doctrine. Read about the persecution of the Albigenses and the destruction of the city of Bezieres where, according to Foxe's narrative, sixty thousand men, women, and children were slaughtered because their own Christian doctrine differed from the Church of Rome. Read about the internal "crusades" against the Cathari Christians and the Waldensian Christians or how both Catholics and Protestants executed Anabaptists simply because the Anabaptists rebaptized converts. And of course, there are the Islamic factions of Shi'ites, Kharjis, Azariqis, Wahhabis, and Madhists, and Sunni Muslims who wage war against each other because of internal religious differences they call heresies.

The list is long, and if the reader is informed as to the politics of the day, he will understand that the concept of heresy is simply a political tool religious leaders use to secure their own positions and the power of the religious institution under the guise of defending the faith of God Almighty in Heaven.

The evil side of religion is there for all to see. Sins of the past continue to project themselves into the present. True believers and organized religions are all guilty of promoting their agendas for political power by using God as their vindicator. In the name of God, Christian crusaders warred against Muslims occupying the Holy Land. Christian sects like the Waldensians and the Albigenses were considered heretics by their fellow Christians and were ruthlessly destroyed as infidels by the papist army. Various Muslim sects waged holy wars against each other and against the Sunni majority. During the same era, hundreds of years before the Nazis of Germany began their extermination of Jews, Christians forced Jews in Europe to live in ghettos and wear badges of shame. During the sixteenth century there were dozens of wars between Catholics and Protestants. Both sides executed Anabaptists.

More recently, Hindu fundamentalists have destroyed Muslim mosques; in eastern Europe, Muslims, Catholics, and Orthodox Christians have fought each other as well as killing thousands of Jews over the last hundred years. The carnage continues. Catholics and Protestants continue to wage war against each other in Ireland. Muslims ruling in the Sudan imposing *sharia* are exterminating Christians and animists in the area. Buddhists and Hindus kill each other throughout the subcontinent of India and Muslim militants continue to wage a jihad the Middle East. Radical Shiite Muslims continue to war against the Sunni Muslims and the Baha'is. The list of war and killing in the name of God begins with Abraham of the Old Testament and continues today.[3]

I find it sad but amusing that any priest, mullah, or cleric really believes that an omnipotent God needs anyone to defend His existence and doctrine from the thoughts and actions of any mere mortal. Of course, the adversary is demonized and becomes a "tool of Satan," which gives the threat much more credibility. This allows the religious leader to wrap himself in the cloak of righteousness as he exhorts his followers to kill in the name of whatever god or doctrine they are "defending." If I need tools such as these to mold men's minds, steal souls,

---

3 Haught, *Holy Hatred*, 14–22, 50, 77, 109, 119.

and undermine God's plan for the universe, I better update my passport to Heaven and pack my bags, because neither side of these arguments has invoked my name as an ally; they always call on God to bless their little adventures. Yet both sides vilify me!

If one challenges and presses a person of faith in a debate over a theological issue that person cannot address logically, the person of faith will insist that the holy passage being challenged is subject to interpretation, is an allegory, or he will simply maintain that some things are the word of God *and must simply be taken upon faith.* If one really pushes, and the true believer cannot provide an answer to questions concerning inconsistencies in his holy book or questions of logic or fact in his dogma, he will fall back on his old standby, "Satan is trying to corrupt me, but my faith will protect me." His mind closes down and the discussion is over. *You cannot debate a religious person with facts because religions are based on certain tenants of faith or tradition that by their very nature transcend logic and fact.*

Unfortunately, most people never independently read a "holy book" with the idea of drawing their own conclusions as to what is written, by whom it may have been written and why, or what it really means. They let priests, clerics, and their affiliated religious institutions do that.

Instead of reading holy books with an inquiring mind, they read instead for confirmation of church dogma. Sunday school and church lessons obviate the need to draw one's own conclusions. Which version of Christ's resurrection and ascension is celebrated every Easter? Is it the version as written in the Book of John? Is it Mark's? Or is it the gospel according to Matthew? The Bible relates more than one version, and the versions differ remarkably. "In dogma we trust" has been the silent cry of the Christian every Easter Sunday for hundreds of years.

And lest you think I am picking only on Christianity, know that Christians do not have a religious monopoly on dogma. Jews have institutionalized dogma in their religion. Muslim leaders twist the Koran to their own interpretations to justify political actions and counter inconsistencies in the Koran. There are no organized religions, major or minor, that are not guilty of promoting dogma or reinterpreting the meaning of their holy books when it suits them.

The greater the ignorance the greater the dogmatism.

—Sir William Osler

Let's Examine Religious Beliefs from My Point of View

All religions are founded on the fear of the many and the cleverness of the few.

—Stendhal

Each of the world's major religions has certain general tenants that its members will agree are basic to the faith. For example, Christians believe Christ was (is?) the Son of God and that he was crucified, dead, buried, and rose from the dead. The Apostle's Creed pretty well sums up the basic beliefs of Christianity. From that foundation of basic dogma, Christianity breaks itself into various sects, each having minor or major differences in interpretation of the faith.

I propose to briefly outline the basic, general beliefs of some of the more widely known religions for those who are not familiar with religions other than their own. To avoid a charge of bias in my summaries (but not my rebuttals!), I reference Joseph Gaer's book, *What the Great Religions Believe*, as well as *The Long Search*, by Ninian Smart, as sources the reader may wish to use to compare my summaries of these religions. As an additional source, I refer you to Huston Smith's *The Religions of Man*. (If you do not feel I have been totally objective, refer to these three well-known sources to verify the basic premises given in my summaries.)

Having properly versed you on mankind's more scholarly and "objective" (i.e., politically correct) approach, I shall then explain in my own words how these same beliefs appear to a nonbeliever or to someone of a different religious persuasion who might read the holy books of each religion without benefit of the interpretive dogma that the respective "body of believers" provide to those who attend their services. As Sir Thomas Browne once said, "The religion of one seems madness unto another." The instinct to stamp out such "madness" is why Catholics, Muslims, Protestants, Jews, and even the so-called pacifist Buddhist and various Hindu sects continue to wage a sometimes subtle but virulent campaign against their respective competitors for political power (first) and human souls (second).

This struggle among the major religions began back during Abraham's time and was present during the rule of Egyptian pharaohs. Religious strife has continued ever since. Early pagans chose their various gods based on local tradition and for specific protections. Each pagan may have worshiped several gods, many of them different than those of his neighbor. But each man's choice of gods was understood and respected by others who knew him. The goal of the polytheist was to incur the favor of his gods. More importantly, the pagans worked hard not to anger or offend *any* of the gods, so tribes, cities, and cultures often adopted their neighbors' gods as insurance against disaster.

But then something strange happened. A man named Abraham claimed to have a personal god who was supreme over all other gods. (We can only assume Abraham was the first monotheist of the Semitics; in any case, he is the one history [the Bible?] has chosen to anoint as the father of monotheism. Actually, a form of Egyptian monotheism predated Abraham, but who's counting?) Gradually, Abraham's personal god, El Shaddai, became known as the God of Abraham.[4] Abraham, the warrior sheik, got along reasonably well with his neighbors and

4 Potok, *Wanderings: Chaim Potok's History of the Jews,* 51.

later with the Egyptians. He didn't have a problem with the fact that they had their own gods. There was a time when religious tolerance prevailed in the Holy Land.

But after Moses assumed leadership of Abraham's descendants, the God of Abraham—El Shaddai (The Unknown), a.k.a. YHWH—became a jealous god. Thereafter, as they emerged from indenture in Egypt and began their conquest of Canaan (promised to them by YHWH), those who failed to worship YHWH or worshiped competing gods were put to the sword.[5]

The cruelty and barbarism afflicted throughout history by organized religions upon nonbelievers and so-called heretics exceeds anything ever blamed on me and the so-called "forces of evil" that I am reputed to command in my supposed quest for world dominion. I would even venture to state that the death, cruelty, torture, and destruction created by religious fervor in the past and still occurring today embodies the evil of organized religion. Religious intolerance has fostered much evil upon mankind, however holy the intent. Later, we'll explore some of these terrible conflicts so that the true believer (if ye are still with us in this reading) can better understand why I maintain my innocence against accusations made against me by certain religions of the world.

> *Think not that I am come to send peace on Earth: I came not to send peace, but a sword. For I am come to set a man at variance against his father, and the daughter against her mother, and the daughter-in-law against her mother-in-law. And a man's foes shall be they of his own household.*
> —Jesus Christ (from the Book of Matthew in the New Testament)

---

5 *The Holy Bible*, RSV, Numbers 25.

Hinduism

Each man is the architect of his own fate
—Appius Claudius

This religion originated in India. It teaches that the world was not created but has always existed and always will exist. It is tolerant to other faiths. It has neither founder nor fixed creed. The central belief of Hinduism is that there is one Universal Spirit, called Brahman, the world soul. Brahman is a god who consists of three components named Brahma (the Creator), Vishnu (the Preserver), and Shiva (the Destroyer). Man is considered as part of the world soul.

Hinduism teaches that man should submit to fate. It teaches that the soul is ruled by serenity and the tranquil search for truth. It teaches also in reincarnation of the soul and the law of karma whereby "from good must come good, and from evil, evil."

Hindus believe in a caste system whereby the priests and philosophers are at the top of the caste and the Sudras are at the bottom. A person belongs to a caste by virtue of birth. The castes worship in different temples, are buried in different cemeteries, and cannot socialize together. Certain lower castes cannot read and study the Hindu holy books, known as the Vedas.

The holy books reflecting Hindu cannon are the Vedas (Books of Knowledge), the Brahmanas (commentaries on the Vedas), and the Upanishads (mystical speculations). The Bhagavad Gita (the Lord's Song) is part of an epic that recites the basic beliefs of Hinduism.

Hinduism consists of a multitude of sects and ancient religions that practice Vedic rites. The larger of these various faiths include Jainism, Sikhism, and Parsees. Jainism might be called the fundamentalists of the Hindu world; Sikhism ties together components of Islam and Hinduism; and Parsees represent the prophetic nature of Hinduism, which has evolved from the ancient Zoroastrianism of Persia.

The Parsees teach that the God Ohrmazd created the world, and the Evil One, Ahriman, is Ohrmazd's antagonist. This reflects the Zoroastrian belief in the eternal struggle between the forces of light and darkness, which by prophecy will end in triumph by the forces of light. Jains are vegetarians as the result of their staunch refusal to take the life of any living thing. Their philosophy assimilates Hindu ceremony with a very austere way of life. Their religion contains aspects of Buddhism, as well.

The Sikhs are an amalgam of Islam and Hindus resulting from the fifteenth century Muslim expansion into India. They believe in one God but unlike Islamic teachings, Sikhs believe in reincarnation. The prime prophet of Sikhism was Nanak, born in 1469 near Lahore. Sikh scriptures called the Granth is considered the ultimate source of teachings for Sikhs. In contrast to the gentle Jains, members of the Sikh religion are the more militant of the Hindus.

The Hindu believes that individual souls, when they become truly pure and good, no longer suffer the endless cycle of reincarnation through the flesh and ultimately reach a state of unity with God, called Nirvana.

Hindu Hades

Sacred cows make great hamburgers.
          —The WHCA Oven, circa 1972

Hinduism is a classic example of the priesthood establishing hegemony over its believers. The Hindu Brahmins have complicated the basic religion over millennia. They have allowed it to evolve into something that promotes a lifetime of misery to the majority of its believers.

A caste system is promoted by the priesthood. Naturally, the priesthood is at the top of the caste and enjoys the benefits that go with being in control of the minds and resources of the Hindu society. The various castes have divided into separate sects worshiping a multitude of different gods.

Hinduism practices and perpetuates religious apartheid among its own believers. The priesthood tells its followers that they are doomed to whatever caste they have been born into. And because they preach that one cannot change one's fate, they tell their believers that they must submit to the lot in life that they were born into. If they live a good life, perhaps their karma will allow them to better themselves in the next life upon reincarnation.

Meanwhile, don't bother to try to better yourself in this world because, as a devout Hindu, you can't. If you are born into a low caste family or as an untouchable, you are doomed to live out your existence in poverty and misery. There can be no upward mobility for the Hindu. What use is an education for one who cannot use that education? The caste system of the Hindus does not allow the lowborn to work in positions designated for those born to a higher caste.

Now, I must admit that the Hindus don't blame me for their misfortunes like the Judeo-Christian-Islamic priesthood does. Bad things that happen to Hindus are simply the result of bad karma. For that I am truly appreciative. However, so that the non-Hindu reader does not misunderstand, I wish to point out that the source of most uprisings and misery in the Hindu world is due to the very core belief of the Hindu religion, which perpetuates the caste system. Millions of people are doomed to poverty, sickness, and misery because Hinduism condones and promotes it. Originally, the system was created by Aryans who, having conquered the subcontinent, created this variation of economic and religious serfdom to maintain their dominance. As it became accepted by subsequent generations, the caste system expanded from four to five, adding the "untouchables" as the fifth caste. This class distinction continues to expand; Hindus have created informal castes within castes.

Those of wealth and political power maintain themselves and perpetuate their dominance by virtue of a religious doctrine that the masses accept as divine karma. A cynical Vladimir Lenin was right when he said that religion is the opiate of the masses.

The Hindu faith is polytheistic, worshiping millions of gods. They dress them and perform ceremonies in honor of their gods. The original Triad has spread to millions of lesser "gods" who are venerated by various Hindu sects. The original four castes created by the ancient Aryan conquerors have been constantly expanding into group of castes and subcastes that now number into the thousands. Each of these caste groups worship their own particular pantheon of gods. Some of the more popular Hindu deities are Shiva, Kali, Vishnu, and the ever-popular elephant headed son of Shiva, Ganesha. While I, Satan, have no objection to idolatry, I suspect that the warrior religions of Christianity, Judaism, and Muslims find the Vedic mythology and Hindu practice of venerating (worshiping?) the various demigods abhorrent. The God of the Old Testament doesn't tolerate competition, and neither do the religions of the Book (a.k.a. the Koran, the Bible, and the Torah). In any case, the Hindu religion is polytheistic. Hindus simply pick and worship a demigod from a very long list of choices, such as Durga, Shiva, Krishna, Vishnu, Indra, Angi, Ganesh the elephant man, Lakshmi, Hanuman the monkey god, or even Shiva's sacred bull, Nandi. These gods are manifestations of the Universal Spirit. They are not considered separate beings, rather they are divine parts of the whole. Something like the Holy Trinity, eh?

Hindus have not been consistent with their beliefs and have reinterpreted their beliefs to conform to changing times.[6] Religions tend to adapt their doctrines to changing times, some more successfully than others. I just don't understand why a doctrine of religious truth and/or fact in one era becomes an allegory or is ignored in another era. If a religion is founded on a doctrine of one God, how can its faithful reconcile to a concept of one God, manifested by a Trinity or a pantheon of demigods? If a religion mixes myth with fact, how can one separate the two? Where is the credibility that sustains the faithful?

But my criticism of Hinduism lies not in its theology. If one looks with a critical eye, the similarities of Judaism, Muslims, Christians, and Hindus are actually quite striking. An obvious example is that while all four religions profess to believe in one God, in many cases they worship proxies. Another example is that they all have a priesthood. Their holy books mix myths and allegory with facts, and one cannot always be certain which is which. They all promote the goodness in man and have their own versions of Nirvana to encourage it.

Nay, I have no quarrel with Hindu theology. They accept responsibility for their actions and do not try to blame me for

---

6 Smart, *The Long Search*, 26.

27

the evil men do. Still, I marvel at man's capacity to tolerate the inhumanity of a caste system that consigns millions of his fellow human beings to a life of starvation and misery simply because of the circumstances of birth. If I am evil incarnate, what do you call Hinduism? I merely tempt mankind and seek to open his mind. Hinduism condemns its believers (at least the lower castes) to Hell here on Earth in this life by virtue of being born. Is Hinduism less evil than I simply because it wraps itself in the virtuous definition of a major religion? What is the difference between Hell in this life and the Hell of an afterlife other than the perceived duration? Their Hell in this life is very real; Hell as promised by religious dogma is abstract, contradictory, tentative, and maybe even nonexistent.

There is in man an up-welling spring of life, energy, love, whatever you like to call it. If a course is not cut for it, it turns the ground round it into a swamp.

—Mark Rutherford

Buddhism

Businesses may come and go, but religion will last forever, for in no other endeavor does the consumer blame himself for product failure.

—Harvard Lamphoon, "Doon" (paraphrased)

Buddhism evolved as the direct result of the Hindu caste system. Disillusioned Hindus found the prospect of thousands or perhaps endless reincarnations to improve one's lot a very depressing situation. A man named Buddha was born in 563 BCE as a prince of a small tribe in northern India.

Young Buddha was raised and educated as a Hindu. He took his vow of allegiance to the Hindu faith and was sent away to learn the Vedas. He became as learned in Hindu scripture as anyone in the kingdom. He later married and began living in the luxury and beauty that a prince of his caste was entitled.

Later in life he realized that there was much suffering and misery in the world from which he had been shielded. He then shaved his head, put on the rough attire of a monk, and left his family in search of enlightenment. The night he left his home is known to Buddhists as the Night of the Great Renunciation.

After much searching and considerable thought, he finally developed the framework of his philosophy. He then went to the city of Benares and preached to the monks there. After the sermon, the monks asked him if he were not a god or a saint, then what was he? He replied, "I am awake."

By the time Buddha was thirty five years of age, he had become known to his followers as "The Enlightened One." Buddha lived to the age of eighty and lived to see his philosophy become a dominant moral force in India and a major reason why Hinduism instituted reforms, which allowed it to regain its earlier hold upon the people.

Buddhism is a philosophy of life and ethical teachings that is comprised of many different sects practicing various rituals, each with different interpretations of the teachings of Buddha. Unlike the Judeo-Christian and Islamic religions, Buddhists have no bible in the sense that the religion refers to one holy book that sets forth its canon. They do, however, have collections of Buddha's teachings, sayings, and sermons. These are known as the "Three Baskets of Wisdom." It is around these teachings and sayings that Buddhism is centered. Buddha's original teachings were devoid of authority, ritual, tradition, theology, ecclesiastical speculation, or religious supernaturalism. Buddha's answer to Hindu fatalism was personal self-reliance.

There are two major differing theologies of Buddhism: "Followers of the Greater Vehicle of Salvation" and "Followers of the Lesser Vehicle of Salvation."

The Greater Vehicle teaches that a man's salvation must involve the salvation of others and that religion is the concern of everyone. It also teaches that Buddha is the savior. Adherents believe in personal prayers and heavy reliance on ritual.

The Lesser Vehicle teaches that each individual must seek and find his own salvation and that religion is the concern of the monks. Its promoters believe that Buddha was a saint and a teacher, but not the world's savior. Ritual and prayer are not encouraged.

There are basic beliefs, however, that all Buddhists subscribe to. Buddhists believe in the Four Noble Truths, the Eightfold Path, the Buddhist Ten Commandments, and the Ten Perfections.

The First Noble Truth is that life is a form of suffering, as well as is death, birth, being exposed to the undesirable, being deprived from one's likes, and the failure to realize one's desires and ambitions.

The Second Noble Truth is that suffering comes from man's desires. These desires include his desire to exist, lust, and other selfish desires. These desires are the source of man's suffering.

The Third Noble Truth is that suffering can be eliminated by the expelling and annihilation of desire.

The Fourth Noble Truth is that man can overcome his selfish desires and find perfect peace by following the treatment contained in the Eightfold Path:

1. Right Knowledge: Reason and belief must be carefully examined before a truth is accepted.
2. Right Aspirations: Seek to improve oneself and aspire toward a higher life.
3. Right Speech: Never lie or slander, be thoughtful, and avoid negative traits, such as coarse language.
4. Right Behavior: Never steal, kill, use drugs or alcohol, or become involved in regrettable activities. Never do anything one may later regret or be ashamed of.
5. Right Occupation: Never choose an occupation that conflicts with Buddhist values.
6. Right Effort: Strive to avoid evil, and work to develop desirable virtues.
7. Right Awareness: Be conscious of one's being and maintain proper self-awareness.
8. Right Concentration: Practice and contemplate the Noble Truths to obtain liberation and enlightenment.

The basic concepts of Buddhism are summarized in the following list:

1. From good must come good and from evil must come evil. This it the first Law of Life in Buddha's teachings.
2. Prayers, sacrifices, and appeals to the gods serve no purpose. To obtain what one would ask of the gods requires that one must follow the Eightfold Path and practice the Buddhist Ten Commandments. One can achieve what one would ask of the gods only through practicing Buddha's teachings.
3. The world has always existed and always will be. There is no "creation" or "doomsday" in Buddha's teachings.
4. People are not created by Brahma into castes. There are only good people and evil people. Unlike the Hindu religion, castes are not recognized by Buddhists.
5. Man has no soul and (in the Western context) is endowed with free will.
6. The goal of life is the end of the "self" and future reincarnations.
7. The chain of reincarnations for a Buddhist ends when one attains perfect wisdom and enters Nirvana.

Buddhism: My Point of View

The most preposterous notion that H. Sapiens has ever dreamed up is that the Lord God of Creation, shaper and ruler of all the universes, wants the saccharine adoration of his creatures, can be swayed by their prayers, and becomes petulant if he does not receive this flattery. Yet this absurd fantasy, without a shred of evidence to bolster it, pays all the expenses of the oldest, largest, and least productive industry in all history.

—Robert Heinlein,
Notebooks of Lazarus Long

Buddha agreed with Lazarus Long. Belief in intercession from the gods is to believe that an omnipotent entity will take sides in a local high school basketball game. Both sides pray for victory; does God cause a tie game? Do both teams win? Did the winning team pray harder or have more faith? Or does the better team win that game on that day due to its own hard work and skills? Does God play favorites?

Buddha preached a religion that contrasts with the six basic traits found in all other major religions. He preached a religion devoid of authority, ritual, theology (speculation), tradition, the grace of God (or gods), and the supernatural. He preached that man has no soul. And he taught that men are responsible for their own actions—no blaming it all on the devil or praying to God to save them from their sins. (Just what I've been trying to tell people for the last few millennium.) Now, what kind of religion is this?

I am always amazed that someone who could walk away from his family responsibilities without a hint of remorse could come up with such noble guidelines for life. Still, I suppose one could argue that while his family may have been distraught and inconvenienced, they did not truly suffer much. Buddha was a prince and came from a wealthy family. His wife and children would have been well cared for in their abandonment. All's well that ends well, eh?

Actually, while I may disagree with some of Buddha's dictates, I have no quarrel with the Buddhist religion as presented by Buddha himself and later written down for Buddhists in one of their holy books, called the Pali Canon. Like Jesus Christ, Buddha wrote nothing down, so even the consistency of his words and teachings is colored to some degree by partisan interpretation and understanding.

I remind the reader: There are no *holy* books in any religion. There are no translations or interpretations of any avatar or prophet's words or deeds that have not been tainted in some way by man. The words you read are simply the words written, translated, and interpreted by men. Some of them had political agendas to promote, some merely made minor editorial changes to suit their own philosophical tastes, and others simply made honest mistakes as they went about their work. The men who translated the "holy" books we now read in any language were simply your garden variety of knaves, clerics, pseudosaints, and sinners. No more, no less.

I criticize only what Buddhism has now become. The philosophy of Buddha has been turned into a religion, and the religion has now gone full circle. Buddha, the atheist, revolted against rite, religious authority, the grace of God, and theologian speculation.[7] Buddhists, (depending on the sect), believe that Buddha himself is either a savior or a saint. The various Mahayanist sects promote salvation by grace, practice ritual and ceremony, and—in contrast to what Buddha taught—continue to cloak themselves in the trappings of an institution. In time, as Buddha's original teachings are revised, reinterpreted, and eroded, like all other major religions, they'll be blaming me for their troubles instead of accepting responsibility for their own thoughts and deeds.

> *A myth is a religion in which no one any longer believes.*
>
> —James Feibleman

---

7 Smith, *The Religions of Man*, 107.

Confucianism

Life is really simple, but we insist on making it complicated.

—Confucius

There are contradicting stories concerning the life of Confucius and his real achievements. Much of his teachings comes to us from the writings of his disciples, who penned such works as *The Annals of Tso* and *The Book of Mencius*. The version of Confucius's life and achievements that follows is just one of many.

In 551 BCE, twelve years after Buddha was born in India, Ch'iu K'ung was born in the Chinese province of Lu. Ch'iu was born under humble circumstances. His father died when he was three, and his mother raised the family. She knew the value of an education and saw to it that Ch'iu received the best education available.

Legend has it that the province of Lu was torn by warfare between rival warlords who contributed to the poverty in the land. Ch'iu observed all this as he studied and resolved to dedicate himself to the study of good, honest government as well as educating the ignorant and poor to help them become productive citizens. He studied tradition, ancient rites and ceremonies, and the Chinese classics.

At age eighteen, he married. He worked at a government post. His home became a meeting place for students and scholars. Eventually he resigned his government post and became a full-time teacher, renowned throughout the province of Lu. Ch'iu, later to become known as Confucius, taught peasants, commoners, the wealthy, and noblemen in a time when only aristocrats and politically connected people were permitted to obtain an education.

During the time he taught, he continued his studies by collecting ancient manuscripts. He is credited for arranging the knowledge he gathered during his life into four books: The Book of Changes (Yi K'ing), The Book of Annals (Shu K'ing), The Book of Odes (K'ing Shih), and The Book of Ceremonies (Li K'ing). His own work, called Autumn and Spring (Ch'un Ch'in) became the fifth. These five books are called the Five K'ing, and from these books he taught his students principles of living, including the following:

1. Courage
2. Judgment
3. Education
4. Self-evaluation
5. Respect and duty to one's elders
6. Friendship
7. Community respect
8. Good government

By the time he was in his fifties, Ch'iu, the teacher and reformer, was recognized as Master K'ung. K'ung, known in the Latin form as Confucius, became chief magistrate of the city of Chung-tu. One version of the legend tells that after a year of working to implement his ideas of good government and education of the masses, he had introduced so many reforms that the city of Chung-tu became famous for its successful government and contented people.

The story continues, relating that Confucius's success came to the attention of the governor of the province of Lu, who then made him minister of justice for the province. One of the first things Confucius did in his new post was to order a study of the prison system and the criminals that inhabited the jails. He found that most of the prison population consisted of the poor and uneducated. The jails were filled with ignorant peasants. The rich were educated, had jobs, and could buy their way out of trouble by corrupting a judge if they committed a crime. Confucius concluded that the solution to eliminating much of the crime in the province was to educate the peasant population. This was unconventional thinking during an age when even the nobility and wealthy did not always appreciate the value of being literate.

He set forth his code of ethics and conduct for the bureaucrats, judges, and legislators to follow. After two years, the prisons were empty. What had happened in Lu became known throughout the land. The ideas of Confucius had proven that they worked in practice as well as in theory.

Unfortunately, political opponents managed to corrupt the governor of Lu, and before long the prisons were once again filled. Confucius, dispirited and saddened by the experience, left Lu in search of another patron willing to let him put his ideas into practice. Unable to find a governor willing to allow him to practice his theories of good government, Confucius eventually returned home and dedicated the remainder of his life to the completion of the Five K'ing. Whether or not each detail of this or other versions of the legend of Confucius are accurate, what is certain is that Confucius taught a code of ethics based on the goodness of man, which has ultimately influenced millions.

According to his student Tso in his work, *The Annals of Tso*, Confucius died at age seventy-three. Estimates of the number of disciples he had range from seventy to two thousand. His former students memorialized him, compiling and writing down all of his sayings. They recognized the value of his teachings and the fact that he had outlined the disciplines and traits of a "superior man." Confucius's primary doctrine was that of "jen," loosely translated as "goodness and humanity." According to Confucius, the superior man has this trait.

Over time, the name of Confucius became obscure. His fame faded, and his teachings were known by few. About a century after his death, a man who became known as Meng Tzu the Philosopher—Westernized as "Mencius"—organized Confucius's works into a volume he called The Book of Analects. The Book of Analects is the most well-known and widely read work for which Confucius is known.

Mencius then went out among the people teaching Confucius's philosophy. Mencius taught that man by nature is good and that evil is unnatural. Mencius's teachings also state that man has free will and freedom of choice and that virtue is its own reward. He quoted Confucius's summary of proper conduct: "Do not do to others as you would not have others do to you." The traditionalist nature of Confucius's teachings can be found in Mencius's teaching that a man's five duties in order of importance are to his sovereign, his father, his wife, his elder brother, and to his friend. The goal of any student of Confucius is to strive to become a superior man.

Mencius declared that the essence of his teachings were the Five Constant Virtues Confucius had set forth years ago. These are the five virtues Mencius preached to the authorities of his day, which can be applied universally to all men:

1. Benevolence: Always keep foremost in mind what is best for the people and those you care for.
2. Goodness: Do not do to your subjects or your fellow man that which you would not want them to do to you.
3. Correctness: Always act with respect and civility toward your subjects and others.
4. Wisdom: Let yourself be guided through knowledge and understanding.
5. Sincerity: Live your life truthfully and honestly.

Douglas L. Laubach

During Mencius's lifetime, the prominence of Confucius, the first sage of China, grew beyond the reputation that Confucius had known during his own lifetime. As Mencius proselyted Confucius's philosophies throughout China, Confucius began to be regarded as the teacher of a new religion. Confucius's once obscure reputation had taken on a new life as the result of Mencius's teachings. Within a few hundred years after Confucius's death, his stature and prestige became greater than ever. His reputation has become legend. Confucius's works have become canonized into a volume called the Confucian Classics. Sacred texts of Confucianism assembled by Chu Hsi in the tenth century CE were the Four Books (Analects, Doctrine of the Mean, The Great Learning, and Writings of Mencius) and the Five Classics (Classic of History, Classic of Odes, Classic of Changes, Spring and Autumn Annals, and the Classic of Rites).

Temples now exist where Confucius and his teachings can be worshiped. The ancient traditionalist philosophies of Confucius are now a religion.

Confucius Say

If we do not yet know about life, how can we know about death?

—Confucius, *Analects*

What I like best about Eastern religions is that they don't lay off the inadequacies of their believers on me. If the believer does wrong, he has only himself to blame. There is none of this "the devil made me do it" routine. They recognize evil as wrong but do not try to blame me for the evils of mankind. I really like Eastern religions.

According to Mencius's teachings, Confucius believed in the innate goodness of man. That is admirable but naive. In the end, Confucius was proven wrong in his assessment of the noble nature of man, and it cost him his job as minister of justice. You see, the governor of Lu who hired him for the job was himself corrupted.

Man may be naturally good, but all men are corruptible, and men of power eventually shed whatever noble nature they might have to ambition as they make their ascent to power. Confucius should have known this. I can categorically state that men of power are not the least concerned with divine retribution. The popes of the middle ages are an excellent example of that. Such men are contained only by the threat of loss of sovereignty to a stronger power that might oppose them or be in a position to diminish that power. Those who are born into power and influence and have never known a life subject to outside restraints, which creates the survival trait of self-discipline, nearly always become evil tyrants. In most cases, even the chance that their endeavors might cost them their lives does not contain their need to achieve absolute power over their dominions. It is an obsession.

So Confucius may have made a grievous error in his fundamental assumption that man is by nature good. And he definitely overlooked the fact that even if man is by nature good, he is always corruptible and subject to change.

One must wonder why the governor of Lu could be persuaded to reverse the noble efforts of Confucius merely to satisfy a few greedy and corrupt politicians and scoundrels. Confucius was highly effective in accomplishing the tasks assigned him. The governor's province was happy, and his own job must have been made much easier by the result of Confucius's work. Could the governor have felt that his own power was threatened by Confucius's popularity and success and thereby allowed a reversal of Confucius's policies to discredit him and reduce his stature? Or more ironic, could the governor's noble nature have been corrupted by Confucius's own success?

And for the record, don't lay this off on "the influence of Satan"; the governor did his thing to Confucius with no help from me. I hadn't even been dreamed up in the minds of men when this happened. It was only later, around 520 BCE that the Jews in the Western world included me in their pantheon in the Book of Zachariah 3:2.[8]

The legends surrounding the romanticized version of Confucius's life do not detail the reasons why the governor of Lu allowed his dominion to lapse back into its old ways. The reference books you can read on Confucius are written by those who have limited source material from which to work. And, of course, it would be unfair for me to outline the details

---

8 Russell, *The Devil*, 190.

of what really happened since I cannot document it. So we are left to make assumptions based on bits of fact, legend, and myth. Remember, however, that in Confucius's time, most rulers obtained their positions by usurpation. Then give thought to what the climb to power or the potential loss of such power can do to the nature of a man. The closer one comes to absolute power, the less noble and more paranoid he becomes.

Still, aside from disagreeing with his fundamental premise that all men are naturally good, I find much in Confucius's teachings that is useful for an orderly world. It focuses upon living in this world rather than living for a life after death. As a religion, Confucianism does not dwell on individual salvation dependent upon subservience to a divine being or its priests, nor does it dwell on disposition of the soul after death or man's relationship with his god. It simply sets forth a code of conduct, which puts a great emphasis on respect to one's elders and tradition.

That Confucius himself is worshiped does the first sage's memory dishonor. Confucius dedicated his life to the pursuit of knowledge; Confucianism as a religion is dedicated to the institutionalism of ancestral reverence. Mencius, like the Christian proselyte Saul of Tarsus, took a living tradition and turned it into a dogmatic creed that pays homage to the dead. During the Han Dynasty (206 BCE–220 CE), Confucianism essentially became the state religion. By the seventh and eighth centuries, temples and shrines to Confucius could be found throughout China.

I find fault with Confucianism as it exists today because it has deified a man who simply compiled and edited ancient manuscripts, incorporating his own commentaries in the process.[9] The man was a brilliant man, but he was simply a man. He was an editor. Neither he nor his works were godlike nor holy. He died a disappointed man because no one would implement his teachings. Why do men turn a kernel of fact into myth and legend and then create heroes who are eventually deified?

---

9 Parrinder, *World Religions*, 319.

Confucius's first book of the Five K'ing was the Yi Ching (also referred to as Yi K'ing, or in English, Book of Changes). It consists of sixty-four hexagrams and eight trigrams that, if properly divined and interpreted, allow the diviner to answer questions he may have about the future. The book gives lengthy definitions as to the meaning of each symbol. There are various ways to come up with the hexagrams, the more common being tossing three coins and scoring them according to values given for "heads" or "tails." After completing the series of tosses and creating the six solid and broken lines that comprise the hexagram, one must consult the Yi Ching to determine the meaning and how it may relate to the diviner.

Confucius held the Yi Ching in very high esteem. To me, it is not much different than numerology, astrology, or the use of Tarot cards to guess at the future. To call it superstition might be too strong, since any type of divination by an adept requires a certain amount of introspection on the part of all parties involved. However, reading tea leaves or the Book of Revelations can accomplish the same results.

To summarize and critique the basic tenants of Confucianism, I offer the following:

Confucius taught the discipline and behavior of the superior man. He never discussed religion or the existence of a personal god. He created an aristocratic code of ethics, which was concerned with the art of government and social morality. His teachings later evolved into the state orthodoxy.

In many circles, Confucius has been credited for works that he did not author. Of the books of The Five K'ing, for example, The Spring and Summer Annals, which cover ritualistic conventions, was not his creation. Nor was the concept of divination through the Yi Ching, which preceded Confucius by generations. Parts of the Analects also predate him.[10]

To his credit, Confucius, in his book of Analects (7.l) admits that he has written nothing original, but simply compiles that which was taught to him or available in his studies through other

---

10 Gaer, *What the Great Religions Believe*, 65–67.

sources. But—as with most avatars—practicing Confucians are not so discriminating, choosing the Confucius of legend over the historical Confucius.

When one peels away the layers of ancestor worship, elitism, and legend, the remainder is not really a religion but rather a guide for the elite and educated to govern the masses. It is as if one lived in a country where only Harvard MBAs could run its institutions. Each of these "leaders" (graduates) would have been shaped, formed, and steeped in the tradition of good old Harvard; through their "Good Ole Boy Club," they would perpetuate their rule and the Harvard culture to the exclusion of all other schools. Solely by virtue of their alma mater, they would be placed in positions to govern and run the engines of commerce. Placement exams would be based on Harvard case studies and articles from the *Harvard Business Review*, written primarily by Harvard graduates.

Consider the parallel between the Confucian bureaucrat and the Harvard MBA. After considerable brainwashing through case studies and administration classes, the MBA candidate learns by rote the standard responses to all the problems that could ever plague any business. Upon graduation, since they now carry the Harvard MBA sheepskin and have become a superior man, they have all the answers (or at least they think they do) and are certified to run any organization in the land.

If the educational process has done its job properly, they will have forgotten how to think for themselves or how to rely on their own deductive reasoning or instinct. To administer the organization or institution (they don't manage, they administer), these highly intelligent beings turned bureaucrats simply need to refer to management theory or a case study for a precedent. And if a valid precedent cannot be found for a particularly difficult problem, they seek out the most recently revered alumni guru for guidance at a higher level.

After a few generations of working the Good Ole Boy Network, following traditional methodology, and engaging in some serious alumni worship and possible myth-making, the

Douglas L. Laubach

MBAs running the institutions of the nation will have thread themselves into the leadership fabric of the country and its institutions. This inbreeding will create a cadre of administrators who will work hard and be successful in maintaining the status quo. And they will be competently mediocre in their positions.

But when the breezes of change begin to subtly shift as a harbinger of radical changes to come, they will still insist on the traditional methods, unwilling or failing to see that the world is rapidly evolving, that they have not kept pace with the changes, and that the revered old ways are not necessarily the best ways today. They will fail to perceive universal changes and the need to recognize them and to function in the world as it is today. They will find comfort in intellectual ceremony, oblivious to the fact that the winds of change are now blowing at gale force. And, not entirely unlike the Harvard MBA's contribution to some segments of American industry in the past, this is what Confucianism has done for religion in China.

But as for me, I have no quarrel with Harvard or Confucianism. Confucianism does not seek to indict me for the woes of the world, and for that I am pleased. It judges me not and I will not pass judgment upon Confucius or his followers. As a wise man once said, "Religions change. Beer and wine remain the same."

Man is the only animal that has the true religion— several of them.

—Mark Twain

Taoism

This is my simple religion. There is no need for temples; no need for complicated philosophy. Our own brain, our own heart is our temple; the philosophy is kindness.

—Dalai Lama

Taoism originated in China sometime in the sixth century, about the time of Confucius. According to legend, Lao-tzu, known as the Old Philosopher, was appointed archivist of the Chinese Imperial Library. His opinions on religion and philosophy became well known to many people throughout the land.

After a lifetime at the library, at ninety years of age, he finally decided to leave. When he attempted to cross the border of the province of Chou, the border guard (whose name was Yin Hsi) would not allow him to pass until he had written down all the essentials of his teachings. Lao-tzu wrote approximately five thousand Chinese Characters divided into eighty-one short poems that became known as the Tao the King (Tao Teh Ching), sacred scripture for Taoists.

Upon completion, the Old Philosopher handed Yin Hsi the writings. After reading the works, Yin Hsi begged Lao-tzu to allow him to travel with him. And, according to legend, Lao-tzu and his first disciple, Yin Hsi, disappeared forever, leaving only the Old Philosopher's little book for posterity.

Two centuries later, a disciple named Chuang-tzu wrote fifty-two books of which thirty-three survive. These books helped interpret, promote, and defend Taoism. We cannot be certain that Lao-tzu even existed, but the existence of Chuang-tzu is documented. Chuang-tzu was to Lao-tzu as Mencius was to Confucius and Saul of Tarsus was to Jesus. And eventually Taoism became established as a religion.

Taoism, one of the three primary religions in China, along with Buddhism and Confucianism, is as vague and indecipherable as the little book that has inspired so many volumes to be written about it.

The essence of Taoism is that the Tao ("The Way") is the path to all understanding. There is the Tao of ultimate reality, which cannot be perceived. There is the Tao of the universe, which represents the forces of all that is. And finally, there is the Tao of harmony of self within the universe. Taken together, these elements of the Tao form an inexplicable philosophy centered around the yang and yin, which is the basis for the cryptic way of life for the Taoist.

A person trying to explain Taoism will refer to the Tao The King (Tao Teh Ching) for insight into the basic beliefs and doctrines of Taoism. But then, rather than explaining the doctrines, he can only recite several poems of the Tao Teh Ching, which tell us really nothing about the beliefs of the Taoist. Sources of understanding attempt to provide explanations of the Taoist philosophy, but due to the ethereal nature of the Tao, they can only speak in metaphors and analogies. As the Taoist will state, "Those who know don't say, and those who say don't know."

However, since scholars cannot even agree on the meaning of the title of the book, Tao Teh Ching (or similar spellings), those seeking to explain "The Way" of the Taoist can be forgiven for failing to summarize the doctrines of Taoism. About all that can be stated with any degree of certainty is that Taoism is a metaphysical system of thought and behavior to establish perfect harmony with the way things are. And there are those who would even take issue with that definition.

The Tao: Inner Peace?

There is no such thing as inner peace. There is only nervousness and death.

—Fran Lebowitz

Taoism is another one of those nonreligions that are actually philosophies on life rather than any belief in God or gods. Since no one can agree on what Taoism really stands for, I question why it is really called a religion. I suppose it qualifies simply because those who have chosen to adopt it as a religion rather than a philosophy have deified Lao-tzu, built temples of worship with their own order of monks, and built a ceremonial religion around reincarnation, rites, divination, and other such beliefs that many might call simple superstitions.

I find it odd that Taoism could ever evolve into a religion, since its very origination is cloaked in myth and unsubstantiated legend. But every religion we have examined or will examine falls into that category, so that should not be a disqualifying factor, I suppose. Myth and legend are common denominators of all religions, and Taoism is no different.

The substance of Taoism as a philosophy is the realization of inner peace and harmony through a metaphysical process that cannot be articulated but is often represented by the yin-yang sign; you simply "know" the Tao when you reach the proper stage of understanding. And as the Tao Teh Ching states, "The tao that can be told is not the eternal Tao."

The Chinese poet, Po Chu-i wrote of the Tao and of Lao-tzu in his poem, "The Philosopher" (and I paraphrase here): "He who talks doesn't know; he who knows doesn't talk. That is what Lao-tzu told us in a book of five thousand words. If he was the one who knew, how could he have been such a blabbermouth?"

Tao as a religion fits somewhere between Buddhism and Confucianism. It also fits somewhere between a philosophy and a religion. It is both, and it is neither. As Tao Teh Ching stated, "My words are easy to understand and easy to put into practice. Yet no one under heaven understands them or puts them into practice." A Zen response to his lament might be: Where is Heaven?

> *We receive three educations: one from our parents, one from our schoolmasters, and one from the world. The third contradicts all that the first two teach us.*
>
> —Charles Louis de Secondat,
> Baron de Montesquiem

Judaism

It seems to me that Islam and Christianity and Judaism all have the same god, and He's telling them all different things.

—Billy Connolly

Judaism has the distinction of being one of the first, if not the first, monotheistic religions of the world. Unlike their polytheist neighbors, the Hebrews worshiped only one supreme god, an immortal whom they named Yahweh.

The Hebrews believe that YHWH (Yahweh, or God) created the universe and the realm of natural existence as we know it. They chronicle God's relationship with the Jews, His "chosen people," in a volume divided into five books, which is known to Jews as the Torah (The Five Books of Moses). The Torah is better known to Christians as the first five books of the Old Testament. They are also known as the Pentateuch (from Greek, meaning "five scrolls").

The Torah tells of the first Hebrew, Abraham, and chronicles Abraham and his descendants through the last days of the Sumeric universal state, telling of Noah and the Flood, Cain and Abel, bondage of the Hebrews in Egypt, the years of wandering in the wilderness by the Israelites, and Moses and the Ten Commandments.

The Torah recites the history and genealogy of the Israelites and records their laws as set forth by Moses. The universal laws delivered to Moses on Mount Sinai by God, known as the Ten Commandments, form the moral cornerstone of over half the world's population. As taken from the Torah (Jewish Publication Society of America, Second Edition, 1976) they are as follows:

1. You shall have no other gods beside Me.
2. You shall not make for yourself a sculptured image or any likeness ... or bow down to them or serve them.
3. You shall not swear falsely by the name of the Lord your God.
4. Remember the Sabbath day and keep it holy.
5. Honor your father and your mother.
6. You shall not murder.
7. You shall not commit adultery.
8. You shall not steal.
9. You shall not bear false witness against your neighbor.
10. You shall not covet.

The Ten Commandments are the rules set forth to maintain order within the Jewish community. These rules were subsequently adopted by Islam and Christianity.

The rest of the biblical Old Testament is divided into two sections, known as the Prophets and the Writings. The Prophets chronicle the various activities of the Hebrew kings and prophets and their impact upon the nation of Israel. The Writings are a mixture of poetry, proverbs, and praises to Yahweh.

The primary tomes of Judaism—defining its belief in one God and its history, rules and traditions—are the Torah, the Talmud, and the Midrashim. Chronologically, the Torah is followed by the Talmud, a vast syllabus of law, history, and commentary that is the basis for postbiblical Judaism. Another Jewish holy book, the Midrashim, is a repository for legends, exegesis, and treatises, which began to develop before biblical canon was fixed and was not completed until the late Middle Ages.

Throughout their literature, the Jews acknowledge man's uniqueness and affirm their belief that God has chosen them above all others to assist in achieving God's will in the affairs of men. They had a covenant with Yahweh: Yahweh would give himself in goodness to His people if they would pledge to keep His commandments. The Jews do not consider themselves superior to others by virtue of race or intellect; they simply acknowledge the fact that they have been chosen by God and are bound by His law. The Bible states the fact openly in Deuteronomy, chapters 6 through 8, where Moses tells his people that they are God's chosen and are bound by a covenant God made with their fathers.

The covenant began with Abraham and was reaffirmed when the Israelites were led out of bondage from Egypt. Much of Jewish history tells of the Hebrews breaking their covenant with God, a prophet warning the Hebrews of the punishment to come if they do not mend their ways, and the subsequent punishment imposed by Yahweh on His chosen people when they fail to heed the warnings they are given.

There are various sects within the Jewish community, which range from the ultraconservative and fundamental to an extremely liberal interpretation of Judaism. There are Orthodox Jews, Reform Jews, Hasidic Jews, Conservative Jews, and others. The common threads between these diverse groups are faith in one God, observance of tradition and custom, and the Jewish identity as a nation.

A History Refresher on Judaism

Thou shall remember the eleventh commandment
and keep it wholly.
—Robert Heinlein, *Notebooks of Lazarus Long*

Sometime after the fall of the kingdom of Ur and before the time of Hammurabi's Babylonian empire, Abraham and his tribe entered Canaan and ultimately settled at the oasis of Beersheba. He had a son, Isaac, by his wife, Sarah, and another son, Ishmael, by his maidservant, Hagar. The dynasty had begun, with Isaac begetting Jacob and Esau, who beget Benjamin, and so on until we get to David, king of Israel.

It is interesting to note that the Arab nations consider Ishmael, son of the Semite Abraham, the father of their people. The Jews consider Abraham, an Amorite, as the father of the Hebrew people.[11] I find that rather odd, considering the enmity the Arabs hold for the Jews.

Unlike the nearby tribes of Amorites, Moabites, Canaanites, Hittites, and other such tribes who worshiped various gods, Abraham believed in just one god. Not just any god, mind you, but *the* God, El,[12] who identifies himself to Abraham, Jacob, and

---

11 Potok, *Wanderings*, 39, 45, 52.
12 Karen Armstrong, *A History of God*, 14.

Isaac as El Shaddai.[13] And Abraham had a covenant with his God, which guaranteed his descendants would be a great people and that the land of Canaan would be theirs. Other covenants with God would follow over the centuries. (I stayed out of these deals, since Yahweh, a.k.a. El, pretty much took care of both ends of the good and evil spectrum in those early days.) Abraham wandered all over the Levant with his herds, building altars to God at different locations.

During Abraham's time, there was a great famine, so he and his beautiful wife, Sarah, went into Egypt where Abraham prostituted her to Pharaoh, claiming her to be his sister. (Yes, it's all there in the Bible. Check it out in Genesis, chapters 13 and 20, if you don't believe me.) He eventually left Egypt with considerably more wealth than he had arrived with. He was now a very rich man. God soon again told Abraham He would give him all the land he could see from where he stood. Later, after the events at Sodom and Gomorrah, Abraham tried to pimp Sarah to King Ablimelech using the same "she is my sister" routine. Ablimelech discovered that Sarah was actually Abraham's wife (and half sister?) and returned her to Abraham along with a bounty of cattle, sheep, slaves, and silver.

By this time, Abraham had fathered Ishmael through Hagar and Isaac through Sarah. The dynasty thus began. Isaac fathered Jacob and Esau. Jacob cheated Esau out of his inheritance. Laban, Jacob's father-in-law-to-be, cheated Jacob out of seven years of servitude in the purchase of Rachel as his wife. Jacob's wives had twelve sons among them all. Jacob (and God) cheated Laban out of all of his livestock. At God's command (either at Penuel or Beth-el, depending on which biblical version one chooses to believe), Jacob changed his name to Israel and God made a covenant with Israel that all He had promised to Abraham and Isaac would be given to Israel and his offspring. Jacob (a.k.a. Israel) settled in the land of Canaan. Jacob's twelve sons became the twelve tribes of Israel.

---

13 Jack Miles, *God: A Biography*, 61, 63.

One of Jacob's sons, Joseph, became second in command to pharaoh of Egypt and helped Jacob's family during a major famine. There the twelve sons of Israel lived and multiplied until the time of Moses.

For a few hundred years we hear nothing about the Hebrews in Egypt. Then we discover that during tumultuous tides of events in Egypt, the descendants of Jacob's clans who escaped the great famine into Egypt were impressed into slavery.

A man named Moses makes a covenant with El Shaddai, who now calls Himself YHWH. Moses ultimately leads the Hebrew people out of their bondage in Egypt. They stop for a brief while at Mount Sinai where God makes another covenant with Moses for the Hebrew people. Laws are set forth by which the Hebrew people will live. They wandered the area for a generation. Moses died.

Under the leadership of Joshua, the Tribe of Joseph's house began a bloody conquest of Canaan. When the fighting and killing were done, the Tribe of Judah occupied the southern portion of the land, from the Red Sea north to Jerusalem. Israel consisted of the northern tribes, located from the Dead Sea to the city of Dan, north of the Sea of Galilee, bordering Phoenicia. Thus the Hebrew nation was divided into two lands: Israel and Judah.

Now at this time, Egypt and the Hittite Empire were the dominant powers in the area. The benign Hittite empire was destroyed when the Philistines ushered in the iron age of weapons and flooded into Canaan. The Egyptians were busy fending off a group of people of unknown origin they referred to as the Sea People. For the Hebrews, it was the biblical time of Judges. Hebrew tribes fought with each other in what amounted to civil war between the tribes. Then, threatened by the Philistines who insisted they lay down their arms, they took up the sword against the Philistines, to whom they were paying taxes.

The Philistines destroyed the Israelite army and captured their sacred Ark of the Covenant. (They later returned it; bad karma or some such reason.) An Israelite judge from the Benjamite tribe named Saul became leader of the northern tribes and first king of Israel. He spent the rest of his life fighting Philistines, Amalekites, Moabites, Edomites, and a host of others. He lost his head to the Philistines, killed by assassins loyal to David, and was replaced by David, from the southern tribe of Judah.

Now King David was as flawed as his predecessor, King Saul. David even sold his services to the Israelites' mortal enemy, the Philistines, for a year as he waged war against Saul. David had Uriah, the husband of Bathsheba, assigned to a position in battle that ensured the man's death so that David could marry the man's widow. David was involved in several unsavory episodes and massacres, including the extortion of wealthy Nabal lest he, David, take the man's wife, Abigail. (David subsequently married Abigail anyway.)

To put it bluntly, David was not a nice man. And nowhere in the Bible am I implicated as the villain who put him up to all this. I could have taken lessons from this guy! David did all this without any help, other than some strong moral support from a couple of local prophets. This reputed ancestor of Jesus the Nazarite was certainly a self-made, evil man. But he was YHWH's chosen, so he got by with things you and I would be cast into Hell for. And in spite of all the terrible deeds David performed, YHWH made a separate, unconditional covenant with this man that his would become an everlasting dynasty for the Hebrew people! And there are those who say the wages of sin are death? They obviously haven't really read their Bible. God definitely rewarded David for his terrible acts against his own people. Ah well, I guess the end justifies the means, eh?

Time marches on. The family patriarch, David, dies; David and Bathsheba's son, Solomon, becomes king. Solomon killed those who were a threat to his throne, secured the empire, gave away a few Israelite cities to King Hiram of Tyre, and died in 928 BCE, leaving a strong, regionally powerful, and wealthy kingdom to his son, Rehoboam. Rehoboam promptly alienated the tribal elders, and the kingdom split in two. Jeroboam was named ruler of the northern land of Israel; Rehoboam, son of Solomon, ruled Judah in the south.

A succession of kings followed for both Hebrew kingdoms of Judah and Israel. The Assyrians conquered Israel (Israel, mind you, not Judah) and moved thousands of Hebrews into various areas of the Assyrian Empire. These Hebrews became known as the ten lost tribes of Israel. The nasty Assyrians replaced the transplanted Hebrews with Samaritans. (I guess we can thank the Assyrians for providing us with the "good Samaritan" of the New Testament parable.)

Meanwhile, to the south, Judah played it smart, paid tribute, and kept itself whole. Time passed, and the Assyrians—the so-called Nazis of the Iron Age—lost their power and were replaced by the Babylonians. In 587 BCE, the Babylonians burned Jerusalem and slaughtered the rebellious Jews, dispersing those they did not deport throughout the Mediterranean. This was known as the Diaspora. Thus ended the Hebrew empire that YWHW had unconditionally promised would be ruled by the Davidic Dynasty.

But wait. The Hebrews transported to Babylon had maintained their identity, their traditions, and their religion. When the Persians conquered Babylonia in 539 BCE, they allowed the Jews to return to Jerusalem.

Alexander the Great swept through history and destroyed the Persian Empire. Now the Jews were becoming Hellenized, assuming the Greek language and some Greek customs. The Maccabeans revolted and forged the Hasmonean Dynasty, which lasted about a century. During this time, two of the most powerful sects of Judaism—Sadducees and Pharisees—had become bitter rivals for the souls of their kinsmen.

The Sadducees were of the more political and priestly class. They accepted the Hellenization of their world, embraced it, and tended to be more cosmopolitan than the Pharisees, who believed in separation from pagans and had a strong attraction to ritual. The Sadducees later collaborated with the Romans and still later participated in the rebellion of Jerusalem against

Rome in 69 CE. All writings of the Sadducees, as well as most Sadducees, were eventually destroyed by the tenacious and persistent Pharisees, who became the dominant sect and won the right to fight against the identified heresies and teach its apocalyptic doctrine to the Jews.

In direct contrast to the Sadducees, the Pharisees believed in the resurrection of the dead, in angels, and that they were the rightful teachers and interpreters of the oral law given to Moses along with the written law he received on Mount Sinai.

The smaller, more conservative Essene sect withdrew into the desert to practice its version of Judaism free of interference from the more powerful rival Jewish sects who were warring upon each other.

Inevitably, the dark shadow of the Roman Empire reached the borders of Palestine. Not unlike the empires that had come before them, the Romans, being natural administrators, felt it their duty to establish dominion and protection over the rebellious land of Canaan. Much of the apocalyptic literature that is in the Bible (as well as some writings that are not included in Christian canon, such as parts of the Apocrypha) was written during this time. The Idumean and forced convert to Judaism, Antipater, was appointed ruler of Judea by the Romans. Upon his death by poisoning at a family feast, he was succeeded by his son, Herod. King Herod, backed by the legions of Rome, ruled with an iron hand. Herod died, and his two sons succeeded him. Herod Antipas became ruler of Galilee, and Archelaus became ruler of Judea, Samaria, and Idumea. Many Jews migrated to Rome, expanding the Diaspora. Rome later appointed Herod Agrippa king of Palestine, and upon his sudden and untimely death, declared Palestine a Roman province to be ruled by a procurator from Rome.

By this time, Christianity, a heretical extension of Pharisaic Judaism, had begun to weave its way into the fabric of Roman and Jewish lives. Tensions grew, James (also known as Jacob), brother of Jesus and head of the Christian community, was condemned and executed under Sadducean law by the procurator.[14] Zealots began warring against the power of Rome. Pharisaic institutions were being purposely assaulted by the local Roman rulers. Rebellion broke out. In 70 CE, the temple in Jerusalem was burned, and the city itself lay in ruins when the Roman legions had done their work. Both the Sanhedrin (the Jewish court that interpreted Jewish law) and the high priesthood were abolished, and the Sadducees had disappeared as a functioning political force. The Jewish state had come to an end.[15]

All of this history leads up to the creation of the sages of a teacher named Yavneh, who would assume the title of "rabbi," or master. The bloody and vicious wars with Rome continued. By 135 CE, Jerusalem had become a Roman city. Judea had become Syria Palaestina. What was left of the Sanhedrin began to consolidate itself and reestablish contact with the Diasporia, the scattered Jews throughout the world. The Rabbis continued to teach and interpret the Hebrew law and tradition.

During this time of regrowth and transition for the Jewish religion, the Christians—who offered their version of apocalypse to Jew, Gentile, or pagan—were becoming stronger politically.

Meanwhile, the Roman Empire continued to experience an inevitable decline resulting in the birth of various smaller empires and kingdoms. Then, in the fourth century of the Common Era came Constantine the Great, newly self-appointed emperor of the Holy Roman Empire and recent convert to Christianity. And for the record, this conversion was not because of any miracle at the Milvian bridge, but because he had murdered his son, his second wife, and other close relatives over a period of time and wanted absolution from his Mithraic Holy Father, who refused. Christianity, however, offered him the tool of baptism to wash away his sins, so he converted, continued his wicked ways until near death, and then, knowing his time was up and he needed absolution to get into Heaven, he had the Holy Catholic Church perform a deathbed baptism. That's why guys like Constantine

14 Potok, *Wanderings*, 286.
15 Ibid., 294.

end up running things; they spot the loopholes. Anyhow, at this point in history, *sic transit gloria mundi,* so passes away the glory of the world.

After Constantine, the Roman Empire continued its decline and eventually found itself broken into smaller, but still very powerful contenders for world dominion, primarily the Byzantine Empire and the Sassanid dynasty of Persia. The Jews found themselves caught between two great empires but managed to survive the long struggle between the two until the Islamic tide washed over the sands of Arabia and Palestine.

Babylonian Jewry, creator and protector of the Talmud, began to decline, giving rise to a Jewish Diaspora in Spain and one in north central Europe (what is now France and Germany). The Jewish people and their laws were split into two distinct geographic areas. More significantly, each of the two principal bastions of Jewry found themselves in the middle of opposing camps: Spain at this time was ruled by the Muslims; Europe was Roman Catholic. So the two groups of Jews continued to coexist with the more powerful religions that dominated their respective worlds. But they had something in common: both Diasporas followed the laws and traditions of the Babylonian Talmud.

Later came the Catholic Inquisitions, a period known by Jews as the wanderings of Europe, false messiahs, and a new European Jewish sect called Hasidism, a Pietist movement that created cracks in the pillars of Talmudic Law and the authority of the Judaic rabbinic leaders. As time marched on, Jews in Europe suffered subtle and blatant forms of discrimination. They frequently lived apart from the general populace in ghettos and were viewed with suspicion by many Christian countrymen.

Some Jews began to talk of obtaining a Jewish homeland—a Jewish state—where Jews could be free to flee from counties that persecuted them. The British offered them East Africa (Uganda), but nothing came of such talk. YHWH's chosen people continued to await the Messiah promised to them by the prophets and continued to immigrate to various nations all over the world, especially to Palestine and America. The Jew's covenant with YHWH seemed more remote with each passing century.

Then, in 1939, Germany invaded Poland, and the Jews of Europe encountered their apocalypse. Partially as a result of Jewish sufferings at the hands of the Nazis, the nation state of Israel was created and the Jews regained their ancient homeland.

> *To what excesses will men not go for the sake of a religion in which they believe so little and which they practice so imperfectly?*
> —Jean de La Brulyere

The Warrior Religions

From fanaticism to barbarism is only one step.
—Denis Diderot

You may be wondering why I recite all this history about the Jews when this advocacy is to defend my innocence in the evils of this world, not to give history lessons. You have already read what conventional wisdom has to say about the theology of Judaism. However, to really appreciate the major flaw in Judaism, as well as in Christianity and Islam, one needs to understand from whence the Western religions come and how these three kissing cousins evolved into what it they are today.

Judaism, Christianity, and Islam are what I call the "warrior religions," because they each are guilty of promoting horrible religious wars to accomplish their respective goals. Each of these three religions used war and violence to accomplish what peaceful proselytization could not achieve. They have each been both victims and aggressors in holy wars.

The Book of Jasher as well as the Old Testament describes the forced conversion and slaughter of innocents in the name of the Jewish God. Christianity used and promoted the feudalistic society from which spawned the awesome papal powers of the Catholic Church and its wholesale destruction of any groups lacking the protection of a strong sovereign and unfortunate enough to be accused of heresy by the church and its feudal supporters. This was followed with internecine religious wars between the various Christian sects and later between Christians and Muslims. The Muslims, of course, conquered the whole of Arabia and vast portions of Asia and parts of Europe. Those who chose not to convert to Islam were offered slavery or death. Many received no choices and were slain as heretics or infidels. And the Muslims fought with each other over just what exactly it was that represented correct Islamic beliefs just as did the Christians. Heresy has no parentage, it seems.

Truly, the warrior religions have a sorry history of intolerance and hypocrisy. Few true believers will argue the facts of history on this topic; instead they merely relegate religious intolerance and holy wars to the past. The Christian will certainly deny his religion promotes hate and death or would ever push its beliefs off on an unwilling populace. The Jew only wishes to be left alone to worship in peace—live and let live, an eye for an eye, and all that. The Muslim fundamentalist will profess that his Islamic leaders follow the Prophet's command from Allah to build an Islamic state that will care for His people. The more moderate believers will assure you that the Koran's harsh punishments for non-Muslims are not to be taken literally. Churches, synagogues, and mosques do not participate in such awful activities in this modern era, they will each proclaim. But such violence is not just a historical footnote to an otherwise benevolent and caring group of institutions. These fierce and terrible wars of religion and covert political maneuvering still rage all over the world today. And Abraham's people started the whole thing.

A "Promising" Religion for God's Favorite People

We have no problems with Jews, and highly respect Judaism as a holy religion.
—Akbar Hashemi Rafsanjani
—Mohammad Khatami
— And Others

Yahweh's first recorded promise (outside of promises to Adam, which were unfulfilled threats) was to Noah. The rainbow was Yahweh's sign of that covenant. (Did rainbows not exist before God's covenant with Noah? Since any high school physical science student knows that a rainbow is due to refraction of light, I wonder if God changed the laws of nature for the benefit of old Noah?)

The original foundation of the Jewish religion is based upon Abraham's covenant with Yahweh. That covenant was a promise from Yahweh guaranteeing Abraham that from his seed would spring a nation. (Yahweh kept that promise.) Circumcision was the sign of that covenant. Moses later entered into a few different covenants with Yahweh, first to get the Hebrews out of Egypt and later to bind the Hebrews to a written covenant with Yahweh (known as the Decalogue, which was a suzerainty treaty based on models of Hittite treaties, also known commonly as the Ten Commandments.)[16] Yahweh promised to Moses and his Hebrew clans the land of Canaan. And through Joshua's generalship, He delivered. The sign of that covenant was to be through individual participation in the remembrance of how Yahweh, using Moses as His tool, saved them from so many threats. Moses's successor, Joshua, even made a new covenant with Yahweh, which reinforced and added to the original Mosaic covenant.

Then, a few hundred years later, Yahweh made still another covenant, this time with David, king of Judah and Israel. To David, Yahweh made a promise (or two, depending on which biblical version one chooses to read): The conditional promise (conditioned upon proper conduct) was that David's house would always rule the kingdom of Israel, which included the tribe of Judah. The unconditional promise was that David's heirs would hold the throne (of Judah) regardless of personal conduct.

Now, this personal promise (privately and/or allegedly?) made to King David is later to become one of the most significant promises of history. Because of this covenant, the Jews later came to expect the Messiah ("anointed by Yahweh" or "king of Israel") from the house of David to deliver them from their troubles and establish Yahweh's Kingdom (i.e., the kingdom of God) here on Earth.

In my opinion, this "covenant" was merely a shrewd political move by David at the pinnacle of his popularity and power to secure his dynasty from future usurpers by claiming Yahweh's support for Davidic kings. From this covenant, which evolved into expectations for a Jewish messiah, came several "false" messiahs (and false prophets) such as Judah the Maccabee, Simon the slave (of Herod), Judas of Galilee, Theudas, bar Kokhba, and a host of others who waged actual wars of rebellion or heralded the kingdom of God in defiance of Roman authority. One such messianic claim was made by Joshua, a carpenter from Galilee.

16 Potok, *Wanderings*, 102–112.

This claim, stemming back to the Davidic covenant, sowed the seeds for a new Jewish sect that ultimately mutated into Christianity. (More about that later ...)

The Old Testament, the Jewish Pentateuch or Torah, is a book of myth, allegory, metaphors, and some old-fashioned but sophisticated distortions of the facts. It copies Egyptian myths using metaphors and often incorporates myths into such stories as the Song of Deborah, Sampson, Joseph, and others.[17] It often tells the same story twice. These differing versions were done to satisfy the political and priestly factions of the day; sometimes the Aaronite priests were feuding with the Moses faction, other times the Aaronites were jockeying for power with other Levite priestly factions. Sometimes the biblical versions were altered to justify Hebrew political factions of both Judah and Israel for political supremacy. At other times the Bible was redacted and used as propaganda to justify and promote Saul's lineage or the Davidic monarchy over the contender at the time. The Torah was used for Hebrew propaganda as well as theology, and the Davidic line of the monarchy ultimately succeeded in becoming the vessel of Isaiah's allusions to a messiah prophesied to deliver the Jews at the time of the Apocalypse. Of course, as we shall note when we discuss Christianity, David's genealogy seems to be open to major debate.

The so-called twelve tribes of Israel are often confused or have significantly different lists of names within the Old Testament. Supposedly, the twelve tribes are represented by the twelve sons of Jacob by his four wives: Reuben, Simeon, Levi, Judah, Issachar, Zebulun, Dan, Naphtali, Gad, Asher, Joseph, and Benjamin. Moses's blessing to the tribes of Israel omit the tribe of Simeon. Ahijah's prediction of a breakup of Solomon's kingdom is unclear as to whether there are eleven or twelve tribes. The book of Judges omits Reuben, Levi, Issachar, and Gad in one citing, and the Song of Deborah names Gilead, Machir, and Meroz, omitting five tribes descended from Jacob.[18]

---

17 Greenberg, *101 Myths of the Bible*, 175, 254, 258, 263.
18 Ibid., 118, 119.

Thus Judaism is based on dubious and politically motivated claims by various Hebrew leaders and prophets of covenants between the Jews and Yahweh. Their history and myths as cited in the Old Testament, the Jewish Torah, are actually a subtle smorgasbord of Babylonian, Egyptian, Assyrian, and Greek gods and mythology mixed with allegory and symbolism.[19]

Jewish history is replete with "deals" between Yahweh and His chosen people. When one peels away all the pious ceremony, tradition, and complex interpretations of the Hebrew Law, the core of Judaism is the philosophy that the Jews are God's (Yahweh's) favored people and that they have worked out a special deal with Yahweh that will provide dispensation to all Jews the rewards that God grants to those who please Him.

There is nothing immoral or evil in this conceit. Other religions share similar doctrines whereby only those of that particular faith will reap God's rewards to the exclusion of all others. At least, unlike many other sects of the warrior religions, the Jews do not claim that they and they alone will be God's beneficiaries come Armageddon time.

My primary criticism of Judaism is that it has evolved from Abraham's belief that his personal god, El Shaddai ("El the Mighty"), was superior to the gods of other tribes and cities. Over time, El turned into a very demanding universal god with human failings and frailties. The God of the Pentateuch was a harsh, jealous, and downright mean God who supposedly had a blind spot for His chosen people. All others of the human race were expendable. And even His chosen people were at mortal risk when they messed up. Abraham knew God as El Shaddai, while Moses was told that His name is Jehovah. Whatever His name, His psychopathic, schizophrenic personality has been permanently recorded in the tomes of Western theology and has taken shape in the theologies of the warrior religions. His nature is the nature of the warrior religions that worship Him.

---

19 Greenberg, *101 Myths of the Bible*, x–xiii, xxvi, 13, 22, 53, 103, 152, 180, 290, 295–299.

So, because of Judaism, mankind is now saddled with this nasty, semiomnipotent, and angry God of the Old Testament. The Jews created Him and His personality over a few thousand years. Religions like Christianity and Islam that are based on this Jewish God of the Pentateuch continue to perpetuate the "angry god" image, so it appears Western religions will be permanently saddled with this Judaic perception of YHWH for the next few thousands of years. No self-respecting prophet would want to alter such a winning personality. Fear of YHWH, a.k.a. Yahweh, a.k.a. Allah, a.k.a. God, plays well in any church, synagogue, or mosque and keeps the faithful faithful.

> *How odd*
> *Of God*
> *To choose*
> *The Jews.*

—William Norman Ewer

> *But not so odd*
> *As those who choose*
> *A Jewish God*
> *But spurn the Jews.*

—T. E. Brown

Islam

Lycurgus, Numa, Moses, Jesus Christ, Mohammed,
all these great rogues, all these great thought-
tyrants, knew how to associate the divinities they
fabricated with their own boundless ambition.
                                           —Marquis De Sade

Sometime around the year 571 CE, a child who would later be known as Mohammed was born in the city of Mecca, located on the Arabian Peninsula, not far from the Red Sea. He was born into the leading tribe of Mecca, the Koerish. His parents died, and the child was raised by his grandfather and later his uncle, Abu Talib, a camel trader and caravan guide. Mohammed's uncle did not see the need to educate Mohammed, so he never learned to read or write. He did travel extensively with his uncle, however, as they worked the caravan trade, and he came to learn about Judaism and Christianity. At the age of twenty, he left his uncle. A few years later, he became the caravan guide and steward for a wealthy widow, fifteen years older than himself, named Khadijah, whom he later married.

For the next fifteen years, he continued to manage his wife's business with great skill. During this period he was able to observe the petty tribal feuding and ponder the idolatry and worship of so many different jinn (gods, spirits, demons) by his tribesmen. Mohammed himself worshiped a god named Allah.

Mohammed periodically retreated to a cave on Mount Hira, located in the Meccan valley, where he would meditate. It was here during the summer month of Ramadan in the year 610 CE that Mohammed was to experience his revelation that he was Allah's messenger. Here he received his command from the angel Gabriel that he should recite the words as a prophet of the one God, Allah. He told his listeners that he was not sent to work wonders, but to preach to the idolaters.

Mohammed continued to receive Allah's messages and recited them into what is now known as the Koran (Qu'ran), "The Recitation," which is the Islamic Holy Book, the Word of God. His message was received by only a few close friends and tribesmen when he first began his mission as a prophet to the Bedouin tribesmen.

Meccan leaders first ignored him. Then they ridiculed him and persecuted his followers. Later, when they began to fear his growing influence in Mecca and came to view him as a revolutionary, they threatened Mohammed's life and forced him to flee Mecca on the night of June 20, 622 CE. He went to the city of Medina where he accepted the role of administrator and statesman. This flight from Mecca is now known to all Muslims as "The Night of the Flight," or in Arabic, the *Hijrah*.

Eight years later, after numerous battles against the Meccans, raids on Meccan caravans, a siege on the city of Medina by the Meccans, and a massacre by the Muslims of their unfaithful allies, the Jews of Qurayzah, Mohammed finally made his triumphant march into Mecca. Followed by thousands of his followers, Mohammed destroyed the idols of the city but forbade looting or killing. Making his way to the temple of the holy Kaaba stone, which had been a focus of pilgrimage and worship by the Bedouin since the beginning of time, Mohammed accepted the mass conversion of the city.

Within the next two years, Mohammed conquered all of Arabia and converted the land to Islam. He died in 632 CE, leaving the expansion of Islam to his successors, who by the next century had conquered northern Africa, Palestine, Persia, Spain, and parts of southern Europe. Had the forces of Islam not been defeated at the Battle of Tours in 732 CE by the French king, Charles Martel, all of Europe and what we regard as the Western world might today be Islamic.

The core of Islamic belief begins with the Koran (translated as "the reading" or "the recital") as the Word of God given to the Prophet Mohammed. The Koran is a collection of Mohammed's recitals and sermons written in the Arabic tongue as given to the Prophet by the angel Gabriel and is considered by many to represent the finest example of classical Arabic prose to be found anywhere. It is made up of 114 suras (divisions) of varied lengths. The Koran we know today is the canonized version authorized during the caliphate of Othman, approximately twenty years after the death of Mohammed. The order of the Koran as we read it today is not in the chronological order that Mohammed spoke the revelations but rather the order is based on length, the longest chapters generally first and the shortest ones last.

The Arab Muslims believe that they are the descendants of Abraham, who with his two wives, Sarah and Hagar, first sired Ishmael from Hagar and the younger son, Isaac, from Sarah. Sarah convinced Abraham to exile Hagar and Ishmael so that her own son, Isaac, would become undisputed heir to the firstborn's much larger inheritance.

So Hagar and Ishmael were cast out into the desert where Ishmael discovers a spring. Abraham heard of this miracle and went to Hagar and Ishmael and built a cubic temple called the Kaaba. Within the Kaaba, Abraham placed a black stone that he had inherited from Adam, who had brought it from the Garden of Eden when he and Eve were expelled. It is toward this black stone placed in the eastern corner of the Kaaba that every true believer must face during prayers.

The city of Mecca grew up around the temple and Ishmael prospered, his offspring multiplying and becoming a nation. Thus the children of Ishmael did come to regard Mecca as the

Sacred City, making pilgrimages to kiss the Black Stone and to drink the healing waters of Ishmael's spring.

But time and the vast distances that isolated the various tribes began to weaken the faith of Ishmael's children and they fell into superstition, idolatry, and rivalry, feuding among themselves and becoming pagans. These were the concerns of Mohammed as he began to ponder the worshiping of so many spirits by his tribesmen.

The basic tenants and characteristics of Islam are as follows:

1. There is only one God (Allah).
2. The Koran is the Muslim holy book.
3. All men are equal in the eyes of Allah, and no man needs an intercessor before God.
4. The soul lives forever, and upon a man's death it either goes to Heaven or Hell, depending on how he lived his life on Earth.
5. There will come a final judgment day when all men will be judged by Allah for the way they have lived their lives.
6. Drunkenness, adultery, and idolatry are sins and forbidden by Islamic law.
7. Charity is a virtue, and acts of kindness are acts of charity.
8. A man may marry up to four wives unless he cannot afford to care for them; then he is limited to one wife.
9. The world belongs to Allah. Any place on Earth where one chooses to pray is holy ground.
10. Fasting, avoidance of pork, and prayer are important parts of Islamic life.
11. Man is responsible for his decisions and his actions and must walk the straight path.

The Koran proscribes other codes of conduct throughout its suras, but they all tend to reinforce the basic concepts set forth above. The Five Pillars of Islam are the guiding principles for each Muslim. These, briefly stated are as follows:

1. Islam's creed, that there is no God but Allah and Muhammad is His Prophet, is to be declared.
2. The salat (ritual prayer) is to be performed five times daily while facing Mecca.
3. Charity toward anyone in need is to be practiced.
4. Ramadan, a holy month commemorating Mohammed's appointment as God's Prophet and his later escape from Mecca to Medina, is to be observed by all practicing Muslims.
5. A pilgrimage to Mecca at least once in every Muslim's lifetime is expected.

The Koran provides not only personal guidance of how to live as a proper Muslim, but it provides moral and legal rules, which carry the weight of law in most Islamic countries. Today it is estimated that over 20 percent of the world's population (over 1.3 billion people) practice the Islamic faith.

Schizophrenic, Prophet, or Both?

Unlike Christianity, which preached a peace that it never achieved, Islam unashamedly came with a sword.

—Steve Runciman

Note that the sanitized versions of Mohammed's life that are readily available to the public make him out to be a virtuous religious leader and statesman. No one wants to bring up the baser side of Mohammed and his religion.

Islamic law as dictated by the Koran continues to approve of slavery and provides detailed rules as to treatment of a Muslim's slaves.[20] (How can Muslims now repudiate slavery without appearing to repudiate the Koran if the Koran, Infallible Word of Allah, says slavery is acceptable?)

Islamic law says that a woman is to receive a lesser share of inheritance than her brothers, two women's testimony is required against one man's testimony, a man can have four wives but a woman only one husband, a woman must not leave the home without being accompanied by a relative, a woman must keep her head covered inside the home, women cannot

20 The Koran, suras 4:92, 33:50, 23:1.

be rulers or judges, and a host of other such discriminatory rules against women's rights and freedom.[21]

There are countless Islamic laws that are out of touch with both reality and the modern world. Generally, Muslims have managed to work their way around the more irrational rules by devising ruses that adhere to the letter of the law but definitely not the spirit of the law.

According to Mohammed, the Koran is God's infallible and undisputable word. Yet it is contradictory and inaccurate at times. For example, sura 50 states that Allah created the heavens and the earth in six days and was not wearied, while sura 41 states that Allah created the earth in two days, added mountains and nourishments in four days, and created the seven heavens in two days. Adding a day of rest or not, the math doesn't quite make it. Only God or a shrewd lawyer could add two days plus four days plus two days and come up with six days! But, of course, in some versions of the Koran sura 41 is translated much differently, and the eight days is reduced to six. The two days to create the earth are omitted, and the math then comes out nicely.

The Hadith, a book of Islamic tradition and law, supplements the Koran. Together, both books represent the unquestionable word of Allah. These confusing and contradictory sacred texts require learned interpretations so that the devout Muslim does not violate God's Word. Thus doctors of law (muftis, mullahs, and imam) called the "ulema" grew into a professional class not unlike the clergy of Christians. Over time, the ulema evolved and became synonymous with the sharia (immutable Muslim law). The ulema ultimately claimed sole authority to provide official interpretations of the faith and of the law. A doctrine called "ijma" was created, which stated that the consensus of the Islamic community (muftis, mullahs, and imam, that is) was infallible and should not be questioned.

So, after hundreds of years interpreting Mohammed's words and deeds, Islamic law is, for the most part, immutably set and cannot be changed. The bottom line is that "divine

21 Warraq, *Why I am Not a Muslim*, 172–177.

and immutable" laws established for a tribe or nation on the Arabian Peninsula fourteen hundred years ago has pretty much ceased its evolution and has not kept up with the changes and advances in physical and social sciences that have occurred over the centuries.

And of course, there is the ceremony practiced at least three and preferably five times each day by the devout Muslim. More specifically, the pious Muslim performs salat five times daily facing Mecca where the Black Stone is housed within the Kaaba. They do not worship idols but pray to a black rock?

The Real Mohammed

No man with any sense of humor ever founded a religion.
—Robert G. Ingersoll

Mohammed's life should be divided into two parts. The first part of his life was during his ministry in Mecca when he was preaching and suffered ridicule and tribulations as he framed his belief in Allah and established Allah's supremacy over the pagan gods of the Arabs. This Mohammed was a seeker who had inadequate knowledge of Judaism and Christianity but was attempting to reconcile the two religions with his own idea of God's message so that he could bring monotheism to his tribesmen. This Mohammed was sincere, tolerant, and forgiving.

Mohammed's given name at birth was Kutam, and he was born into Mecca's leading tribe. As stated earlier, he was illiterate and his early years were spent learning the caravan trade. Then, several years after marrying the wealthy Khadija, he got religion. Mohammed worshiped the god, Allah, which was considered one of the stronger and more influential gods known to the Arabic tribesmen around Mecca. For thirteen years, Mohammed preached and proselytized in and around Mecca, proclaiming himself to be the Messenger of God. In the last three years of this period, Mohammed had sought refuge from many of his tribesmen and detractors in his uncle's castle near Mecca and was living in the stronghold.

In the year 619, Mohammed's first wife, Khadija, died. She had been his closest companion, his major confidant, and his most constant source of spiritual support. She had been his only wife, and her death was a major loss to Mohammed. Later in the same year, thirteen years after Mohammed began his mission, his uncle, Abu Talib, a powerful clan leader and loyal supporter (but a nonbeliever), died. The death of Abu Talib marked a major period of transition for Mohammed. In the future, clan protection that came with his uncle's unwavering loyalty would not be available to Mohammed.

Medina, a rival trade center to Mecca, soon thereafter became Mohammed's new source of protection and power. Unlike Khadija and Abu Talib, the people of Medina could not act as conscience, confidant, companion, and mentor to Mohammed. No group or person in Medina could exhibit the moderating effect that his first wife and his uncle had on Mohammed. He was no longer restrained by their presence or by Quraysh tribal tradition. Mohammed was now answerable only to his god, Allah.

The second phase of his life as a prophet, during his ascendency to political and financial power, represents the life of a different Mohammed, a life without benefit of advice and counsel from his first wife, Khadija, and his uncle, Abu Talib. This Mohammed was a corrupt and ambitious Mohammed who wielded power as ruthlessly as any tyrant in history.

Whatever tribal ties Mohammed felt for his Quraysh tribesmen became subordinate to his desire to demonstrate and prove that he was God's messenger and to his personal desire to retaliate against those who had for so long humiliated him. This desire for revenge was the forerunner of other character failings and less than moral acts carried out by Mohammed. Mohammed had become a driven man with absolutely no restraints on how he would conduct his mission.

By his own words, Mohammed's actions are justified as revelations from God, not from me. They (with perhaps with the exception of the Satanic Verses) are not inspired by me. Thus the evil deeds of Mohammed are not to be laid at my hooves. I only recite the acts of Mohammed as history has recorded them.

Obviously, I need to dismiss my public relations staff and hire God's PR firm, because had I been in any way connected with such evil and vile doings as was Mohammed, pages upon pages of vilification against me would be written, confirming and reaffirming the fact that I am evil beyond redemption. Had not Mohammed given God credit and justified his acts in God's name, I am certain I would have been blamed for this slaughter. These same acts committed under my aegis could never have been justified to humanity, regardless of the "necessity." Does the end justify the means only when the cause is of a "holy" nature? And who determines which causes are holy and which are not?

One of the first things Mohammed did when he assumed his leadership role in Medina was to send out raiding parties to rob passing caravans of their trade goods. Initially, his raids were less than successful. His first major success occurred when he sent out a party during the pagan sacred month of the Meccans (known as Ramadan), when fighting was not permitted. Even the Medinans were astonished that Mohammed would profane the pagan sacred month. But Mohammed took his one fifth of the booty and ransomed the prisoners, and the Medinans, encouraged by the success of the raid, agreed to continue raiding caravans.

Now don't get me wrong; I understand Mohammed's need to build up a fighting force and keep them paid. It is an ancient devise of kings and generals to pay the fighting men of one's army with the loot of their conquests. I do, however, find it hard to reconcile Mohammed's actions of robbery and murder with his early (Meccan) teachings.

Medina was a city founded by Jews but was inhabited by pagan Arabs and several Jewish tribes. Mohammed at first thought he might convince the "People of the Book" (Jews) to welcome him as their Messiah. When that didn't quite work out, he began to grow suspicious of them, tolerating them only because he was not strong enough to rid himself of them.

During this period, the raids continued and his closest followers prospered. Mohammed began to rid himself of anyone or any group that might oppose him. He established an intelligence network that provided him with information against his enemies. Thus armed, Mohammed began a series of assassinations. These were justified as what one today might call "preemptive strikes." The victims, however, didn't really pose much threat to Mohammed.

Anyone who has read the history of Mohammed and his sufferings during his Meccan period knows that he was humiliated and abused by his own Quraysh tribesmen. The Christian thing to do after he won his victory at Mecca was to forgive his enemies and let bygones be bygones. But, of course, Mohammed was neither a Christian nor a pacifist. And he exceeded the Jewish rule of "an eye for an eye and a tooth for a tooth."

Mohammed had the poetess Asthma bint Marwan of the Aws tribe in Medina murdered because she openly showed her disdain for Islam and Mohammed. (I suppose heresy is as good an excuse as any to justify killing an old woman.) He had Abu Afak, an old man of the Khazraj, murdered in his sleep. Abu had written verses that were critical of Mohammed; Criticism equals heresy equals death, judging from Mohammed's actions and a literal interpretation of certain verses in the Koran (sura 8:68). Mohammed called for deliverance from the oratory of Kab ibn al-Ashraf, a poet of the Jewish Banu Nadir tribe, during a public prayer. Mohammed was delivered from the threat of Kab when several Muslims tossed Kab's head at Mohammed's feet.[22] Mohammed justified his murders, but then most murderers have both a motive and an excuse.

During this period, Mohammed's confidence and strength had grown considerably. Soon he was ready to deal with the

---

22 Warraq, *Why I am Not a Muslim*, 94.

Jewish problem. After experiencing a serious defeat by the Meccans at the battle of Uhud, Mohammed struck against the Jewish tribe of Banu Nadir. They were besieged and finally agreed to leave Medina. The Muslims divided their lands. Later the Meccans launched an attack against Medina. The two-week siege was known as the Battle of the Trench. By this time the only remaining Jewish tribe left in Medina was the Banu Qurayza. After the battle, Mohammed questioned their loyalty and seized them. They agreed to surrender, assuming they would be allowed to leave Medina, forfeiting their wealth to the Muslims. In an unfortunate (for the Banu Qurayza) set of circumstances, Mohammed allowed all the men of the tribe to be put to death, the women and children sold into slavery, and the spoils divided by his army.

Another group of the Jewish Banu Nadir settled at an oasis named Khaybar. Mohammed had the chief of the tribe, Abi 'l Huquyq, assassinated as he slept. Then under a flag of truce and a promise of safety to their new leader, Usayr Zarim, he had Usayr Zarim and his escort of thirty unarmed men murdered on the road to Medina.[23]

In addition to murder and assassinations, Mohammed developed a taste for polygamy. While Khadija was alive, Mohammed never had another wife. But this Mohammed was not the same man that had relied upon his trusted wife's unwavering support and her belief that he was the Messenger of God. During his lowest moments, it had been Khadija that had helped him stay the course. Things had changed for Mohammed now that he had succeeded in his mission. He was no longer the struggling prophet; he was a powerful warlord and self-proclaimed holy man with no one to help him control his baser instincts. The Mohammed of Medina had taken several wives since the death of Khadija and struggled to keep peace within his harem. Mohammed, at age fifty-three, married one of his wives, Aisha, when she was nine years old. Another wife was divorced from her husband, a devout Muslim, so she could wed

---

23 Warraq, *Why I am Not a Muslim*, 98.

Mohammed. Another was the daughter of a chieftain slain by the Muslims.[24] He frequently had "revelations" that justified many of the problems he created regarding his wives and concubines.

This, then, is the Mohammed of Medina and founder of Islam. This is the author of the Koran, which includes many verses such as sura 9:4, "Proclaim a woeful punishment to the unbelievers, except those idolaters who have honored their treaties with you and aided none against you." (For Mohammed, military strategy took precedent over religious principles.) "When the sacred months are over slay the idolaters wherever you find them. Arrest them, besiege them, and lie in ambush everywhere for them...."

While Hell could use men like Mohammed, I must cast my net elsewhere because God has promised Mohammed and his true believers an afterlife in Paradise. I only get those whom Allah sends me. Of course, according to the Koran, that includes just about everyone else: Jews, Christians, infidels, pagans, and any other nonbelievers. I'll probably have to petition Heaven for a permit to expand Hell to make room for all of these souls.

As the religion of Islam assumed its final shape, good and bad took on a meaning distinct from the Judaic or Christian creeds. The Islamic idea of good and bad lost any moral or ethical significance as to whether a deed was morally or ethically right or wrong. Instead, the issue that determined good and bad for the Muslim was whether or not it was permitted by the Koran or by traditional Islamic law. Killing violates the Judaic and Christian creed and their holy books specifically forbid the act of murder. (Of course, this doesn't stop them from such acts, but their religions are at least on record as being against murder.) For the Muslim, however, if approved by recognized Islamic authority, killing can be not only good but the act of not killing could be deemed an act against Islam, especially if the victim was an apostate of Islam or was labeled a blasphemer.[25]

---

24 Warraq, *Why I am Not a Muslim*, 99.
25 The Koran, suras 8:12, 8:38–40, 9:5, 9:27, 9:39, 9:73, 22:9, 47:4.

In sura 9:5, the Koran expressly directs the Muslim, "Slay the idolaters wherever you find them." Other such urgings are found in the Koran under sura 22:9, which says, "As for the unbelievers, for them garments of fire shall be cut and there shall be poured over their heads boiling water whereby whatever is in their bowels and skins shall be dissolved and they will be punished with hooked iron-rods." Sura 47:4 states, "When you meet the unbelievers, strike off their heads; then when you have made wide slaughter among them, carefully tie up the remaining captives." Sura 8:15–16 reads, "Believers, when you meet the unbelievers preparing for battle do not turn your backs to them lest you incur the wrath of God and Hell shall be his home; an evil dwelling, indeed." Sura 8:12 states, "I will instill terror into the hearts of the infidels, strike off their heads then, and strike off from them every fingertip."

These and other suras found in the Koran pretty much sum up the Muslim creed. And to those who accuse me of being deceitful and self-serving, let me tell you how Mohammed handled any contradictions he might have set down in his Koran. He simply abrogated certain verses with a new sura that better suited his tastes at the time. Sura 2:105 states, "Whatever verses we cancel or cause you to forget, we bring a better or its like."

An unschooled reader may not even know which sura is abrogating which, since the Koran is written in the order of the length of the suras rather than in chronological order. I venture to say that the bulk of such contradictions found in the Koran stem from "revelations" during Mohammed's more benign Meccan period being abrogated during his intolerant Medinan period.

So, remember then that Mohammed—who proclaimed more than once in the Koran that I, Satan, am the sworn enemy of Islam—established the religion known as Islam by the use of war, robbery, murder, and treachery. His actions during his reign as God's Messenger suggested he displayed at least three of the seven deadly sins (Catholic, and not applicable to a Muslim, I suppose). To accomplish his mission, Mohammed used means normally attributed to me and my alleged legions in Hell, yet he is revered by millions. I am impressed!

The epic of Islam is a play written by God and Mohammed; I was not invited nor did I take part in this frenzy of empire building. The murders of old men and women and the massacres of Jews, pagans, and "nonbelievers" caused by Mohammed's petty retribution and displays of power are between Mohammed and God. The Koran, purported to be God's divine word, justifies these action. Alas, I missed this party.

Mohammed believed in angels, demons, the evil eye, charms, omens, and other supernatural beliefs that harken back to his earlier years in pagan Mecca. In sura 72, entitled "The Jinn," (shadowy demons, hostile and sometimes benevolent spirits) the Koran references Mohammed's belief in the existence of such beings. Several other suras reference and reinforce Islamic belief in jinns.

Sura 15 explains that the angels were created by God from smokeless fire. Next, man was created from clay and loam. Sura 15:32, in God's own words, relates how I would not prostrate myself to Adam (did God not command all to worship only Him?) and how God reprieved me from his curse until judgment day (at which time the original sentence is to end, and I assume His curse will be lifted—at least that's how I understood our arrangement). During this time, He agreed that I should tempt and seduce mankind on Earth, except for God's faithful servants. *God allowed me no power over His servants; I was granted power only over sinners who will follow me.*

Now this arrangement should give no one other than sinners any problems. If you are faithful and free of sin, I am not allowed any power over you. Thus I have no power to persuade, no power to successfully tempt you, nor any other power to corrupt you—if you are God's servant. Otherwise, God has dictated that as a sinner you must go to Hell. (Keep in mind that this Hell thing wasn't my idea; it was God's.)

The Satanic Verses

We may not pay Satan reverence, for that would be
indiscreet, but we can at least respect his talent.
                                        —Mark Twain

Since I have power only over sinners, there is an incident for
which I am blamed as the instigator but am innocent. It is
well documented by extremely credible Muslim sources. Let me
share this unfortunate turn of events with you.

During the early years of his mission, Mohammed was
trying to reach a compromise with the Meccans. He received
one of his revelations, which told him that three of the Meccan's
most popular deities (al-Lat, al-Uzza, and Manat—all three
considered to be daughters of God) could be designated as
divine entities that could provide intercession with God. (Out
with monotheism; in with polytheism and idolatry!) Later, when
Mohammed realized this hadn't been a very good idea, he had
additional revelations that canceled the verses of exaltation to
these Meccan goddesses.[26]

Sura 53 originally exalted these three goddesses. But shortly
thereafter, Mohammed was told by the angel Gabriel that the
verse exalting the three should have read that it was unfair for
humans to have sons and for God, only daughters. al-Tabari, a

---

26 Armstrong, *Muhammad: A Biography of the Prophet*, 108–113.

devout Muslim historian, and al-Waqidi, one of Mohammed's biographers who lived during the ninth century, have both been cited as reliable sources of this. Sir William Muir wrote a biography of Mohammed and related this incident as "The Satanic Verses," because I was blamed for putting words in the Prophet's mouth.[27]

How could I have had any power over Mohammed when God granted me power only over sinners? The Koran, in sura 15:33, says, "He (God) replied: 'This is the right course for Me. You (Satan) shall have no power over My servants, only the sinners who follow you.'" Concerning the so-called Satanic verses, Mohammed may have spoken in error, but it wasn't because of me; perhaps it was the jinn talking.

> I had no authority over you except to call you, but you listened to me: then reproach not me, but reproach your own souls.
>> —Iblis (a.k.a. Satan) from the Koran,
>> sura 14:22

Christianity

Eskimo: "If I did not know about God and sin, would I go to hell?"
Priest: "No, not if you did not know."
Eskimo: "Then why did you tell me?"

—Annie Dillard

Christianity is divided into three primary groups: Orthodox Eastern Church (one hundred sixty million followers), Roman Catholic (one billion followers), and Protestant Christians represented by dozens of different denominations (one billion followers). These figures are approximate and will change over time but are representative of the fact that Christianity, combining all denominations, is the largest religion in the world.[28]

The Protestant Christians in Europe and North America are divided into many denominations, including Baptists, Lutherans, Methodists, Mormons, Pentecostal, Episcopal, Anglicans, and others too numerous to break out in detail.

Christianity's history begins with the virgin birth of a child born to Joseph—listed in the New Testament in the Book of Matthew as a twenty-eighth generation descendent of King David—and Joseph's wife, Mary. Approximately 5–7 BCE, Jesus

---

28 *The World Almanac & Book of Facts*, 698.

of Nazareth was born in a cave near the town of Bethlehem. Very little is known of his youth.

Jesus of Nazareth was a Hebrew and spoke the Hebrew language. In his language, his name was Yeshu. He was raised as a Jew and was well versed in the books, laws, and prophecies of his people. Like his father, Joseph, he was a carpenter and practiced his trade near and around the town of Nazareth in the province of Galilee. At the (approximate) age of thirty, he was baptized in the Jordan River by John the Baptist and began his ministry, which at most lasted three years.

Jesus preached around the immediate countryside, healing the sick and attracting followers and disciples. His teachings and customs were unlike the normal sermons the people were accustomed to; he taught in parables and mingled freely with the poor, the wealthy, and the sinners. While the basis for all of Jesus's teachings can be found in the Old Testament of the Bible and the Jewish Talmud, he focused the content of his teachings toward the common people, preaching forgiveness and love, repentance, and that the kingdom of God was at hand. The New Testament of the Bible, which records the history and chronicles the life and acts of Jesus and his disciples, recites the various sermons and parables told by the Nazarene.

The Jews still waited for a messiah to rescue them from the evils of the world. Jewish prophecy stated that the Messiah, preceded by the prophet Elijah, would be of the house of David from the city of Bethlehem and would triumphantly enter Jerusalem riding a donkey (Zechariah 9:9).

In fulfillment of that prophecy, Jesus entered Jerusalem to celebrate the Feast of the Passover riding a donkey. He entered the Jewish Temple of Jerusalem and drove the money changers from the temple. This enraged the Jewish priests, who conspired against him. He was arrested on the Mount of Olives in Gethsemane by the guards of the high priest, Caiaphas. The chiefs and elders pronounced a death sentence upon him and took him to the Roman governor who ultimately passed sentence upon him to be crucified for treason.

Jesus was crucified by the Romans at Golgotha. His body was properly cleansed, prepared, and entombed in a vault owned by Joseph of Arimathea, who was a disciple of Jesus. A large stone was placed at the entrance of the tomb and guards were subsequently placed at the tomb. Three days later, two female followers of Jesus went to the tomb and discovered the body of Jesus gone.

Jesus later appeared to the disciples and, before departing, instructed them to preach repentance and forgiveness in his name to all nations. The resurrection of Christ the Messiah was complete.

The early Christians were persecuted by the Romans as well as their fellow Jews. They were persecuted by the Jews as a minor Jewish cult that worshiped a false messiah. They were persecuted by the Romans because they refused to acknowledge the emperor as a god.

A Jew named Paul of Tarsus, who was also a Roman citizen, was one of the Jews sent to deal with the Nazarene sect later to be called Christianity. Paul was among those responsible for Christianity's first martyr, the leader of the Nazarenes, whose name was Stephen. After the stoning, the church was destroyed and many of its members sent to prison. Next he visited the Samarian Jews and then proceeded to Damascus where a growing Nazarene following among Jews was taking place.

On his way to Damascus, Paul experienced a mystical conversion to the gospel of Christ. He became a leading missionary for the small Jewish sect. Up until the arrival of Paul, the Nazarene sect considered itself Jewish and preached only to Jews. Eventually, however, after some differences arose between Peter and Jesus's brother James, Paul began to preach primarily to Gentiles. By changing certain tenets of the Jewish Nazarene sect, Paul established a completely new religion, which we now know as Christianity.

In the year 312 CE, Constantine defeated Maxentius at the battle of the Milvian Bridge, became emperor of the western empire with Licinius ruling in the east, and subsequently converted to Christianity. Later he became sole ruler of the empire. Constantine provided major concessions and funding to his chosen religion, Christianity. He oversaw church canon and supervised the first ecumenical council of the Christian Church, the Council of Nicaea, which by most accounts was attended by 220 bishops, mainly Greek. Due to the Roman Emperor Constantine's nurturing of the Christian Church, it began to prosper and grow into ascendency.

While Christianity has split into hundreds of sects since the beginning of the early church, there are certain core beliefs central to the teachings of all Christians:

1. God is the creator of all things.
2. Jesus Christ is the Divine Son of God.
3. The Trinity of the Father, Son, and Holy Ghost are one entity.
4. Jesus Christ was crucified and rose on the third day, ascending to Heaven.
5. Jesus is the Messiah sent to redeem mankind.
6. Man is born with the original sin of Adam and is thus born a sinner and must be saved or redeemed before he can be accepted into Heaven. Remission of sins requires baptism and repentance.
7. The Gospels of the New Testament are historically true. The Bible, comprised of both Old and New Testaments, is the holy book.
8. The soul is immortal; those who believe in Christ and follow his teachings, repenting of their sins, will enter the kingdom of Heaven and have everlasting life.
9. The Golden Rule given from Jesus is, "Do unto others as you would have them do unto you."

The essence of Christianity is that all followers who believe in Christ and repent of their sins will save their immortal souls and spend eternity in Heaven.

For Christ's Sake

(Satan's Rebuttal of Christianity)

Faith is much better than belief. Belief is when someone else does the thinking.
—Buckminister Fuller

From El Shaddai, God of Abraham; to YHWH, God of Moses; to Christ, the embodiment of God the Father and the Holy Ghost (whatever this Trinity stuff means . . .), we have a lineage of deities that is purported by Christians to be one and the same. According to Christian theology, Christ is not only the son of God, He *is* God. He was born of the Virgin Mary, crucified, died, and rose from the dead on the third day. After a brief stay on Earth to make sure His disciples got the message, He ascended into Heaven and sits on the right hand of God.

Christ knew what He meant when, according to the Book of Matthew (chap. 10:34–36), He said, "Think not that I am come to send peace on Earth: I came not to send peace, but a sword. For I am come to set a man at variance against his father, and the daughter against her mother, and the daughter-in-law against her mother-in-law. And a man's foes shall be they of his own household." Religious history certainly bears out the truth of this prediction. Remember, this is your good buddy Jesus talking, not me.

To better understand why I take issue with Christian dogma, we need to examine some of the misdirection and clues available to us that might put a different perspective on who Jesus was, church doctrine, and how Christianity became what it is. Reams of material have been written on these subjects, so we'll only highlight the most obvious, picking the subjects most easily verifiable by anyone who is motivated enough to check out a few biblical facts. I recount this evidence because it is important that the true believer as well as the intellectually curious realize that the story of Christ as handed down by our church fathers is fraught with contradictions, omissions, errors, inconsistencies, and purposeful misdirection.

Most scholars agree that the Synoptic Gospels (Matthew, Mark, Luke) weren't written by the apostles for which they are named nor are they in chronological order as written. The author of each of the four gospels had his own agenda at the time the respective gospel was written, and that agenda can generally be determined by the attentive reader.

The early Christian communities were split into three primary groups. The *Aramaic-speaking Jews* of Palestine believed that Jesus was the prophet of God and would return during the second coming at the end of time as the Messiah. These were the people to whom Jesus ministered, and they believed that the end of time was imminent in their lifetimes. The *Greek-speaking Jews* were of a later period and realized the end of time and second coming was not as imminent as originally expected. Their beliefs evolved to fit the circumstances, and they came to believe that Jesus was already the Christ and that He was ruling in Heaven. The *Greek-speaking Gentiles* appropriated the central tenants of early Christianity and then vastly expanded the theology of Christ, adding layers of complex doctrine to the Christian edifice. They basically believed that Jesus preexisted as

God before He came to Earth as a man, was crucified, ascended, and was currently sitting upon the throne of God.[29]

The author of Matthew wrote toward the Jewish audience shortly after the destruction of the temple at Jerusalem in 70 CE and wanted to present Jesus as a latter-day Moses with new laws to replace or in some cases supplement the old laws of Judaism. The author of Matthew went to considerable effort to show that Jesus fulfilled Jewish prophecies concerning the Messiah. The Golden Rule and the Sermon on the Mount were the cornerstones of the "good news" that freed Christian Jews from the burdens of Jewish ritual.

Mark is regarded as the earliest of the four gospels, written in Greek but with Aramaic forms of expression, during the time of Nero's persecutions of the Christians, around 64 CE.[30] Mark is a primary source for the author of Luke. The author of Mark was the first gospel author to put oral tradition of the life of Jesus of Nazareth down in writing for the average Jewish-born Christian. He called his writing the Gospel, which means the "Good News." Mark's Good News was that Jesus was the Messiah who preached a new covenant between God and man. By Mark's accord, Jesus was a humble Galilean born in Nazareth who was the Messiah. Mark's gospel details no virgin birth, no Davidic genealogy, and no Ascension.

Luke's letter to Theophilus was penned to make it very clear that Jesus ranked above John the Baptist and went to lengths to differentiate between the two prophets and demonstrate the unfolding of a divine plan. The author of Luke (a Gentile who is suspected of also writing the Book of Acts) wrote to the Hellenized and pagan Gentile audience sometime after the destruction of the temple. He attempted to connect Jesus's words and deeds to the early church. He also wrote to distance the early Christians from Jews, who were not exactly in the good graces of the Romans at the time because of a Jewish revolt in Judea. Christianity had by this time developed from a heretical

---

29 Sheehan, *The First Coming*, 12–13.
30 Asimov, *Asimov's Guide to the Bible*, 903.

Jewish sect to a more universal religion competing with other "savior" religions of the Roman world.

The fourth gospel, John, differs significantly from the synoptic gospels by the fact that it focuses more on Jesus at Jerusalem rather than his teachings to the common folk of Galilee. It portrays Jesus from the perspective of a theologian rather than an evangelist. It is more mystical and somewhat doctrinaire. The Gospel of John was written at least a generation after the Romans destroyed the temple at Jerusalem, perhaps a hundred years after the birth of Christ. By this time, the early Christians were beginning to work out church doctrine and refine their theology. John's gospel helped to provide a framework for future church canon.

With an abbreviated understanding of what the first four gospels were and for whom and when they were written, we can examine a few issues related to the credibility of the New Testament. Let us start at the beginning of our story, the birth of Jesus.

> *A person constantly exposed to an idea or doctrine will, more likely than not, adopt that belief or at least be highly influenced by it.*
>
> —Zog

Virgin Births and Prophecy

With most men, unbelief in one thing springs from blind belief in another.
—Georg Christoph Lichtenberg

The Old Testament book of Isaiah 7:14 (KJV) states, "Therefore the Lord himself shall give you a sign. Behold, a *virgin* shall conceive, and bear a son, and shall call his name Immanuel." The Revised Standard Version cites the verse as: "Therefore the Lord himself will give you a sign. Behold, a *young woman* shall conceive and bear a son, and shall call his name Immanuel." The new Revised Standard version of the verse goes like this: "Therefore the Lord himself will give you a sign. Look, the *young woman* is with child and shall bear a son, and shall name him Immanuel." This verse is one of the more quoted verses that is supposed to be a prophecy for the Messiah of the Jews. The actual Hebrew Translation of Isaiah's words reads, "Behold, a *young woman* is with child and bears a son and calls his name Immanuel."

Matthew 1:23 (RSV) quotes it as, "Behold, *a virgin* shall conceive and bear a son, and his name shall be called *Emmanuel*." (I suppose the spelling of "Immanuel" should not be an issue here, but for the sake of accuracy it should be noted that in the Old Testament Revised Standard Version and King James Version it is spelled with an "I." In both the the New Testament Revised Standard Version and New Revised Standard version, it is spelled with an "E." How about those Greeks?)

But more to the point, all versions of the Matthew verse cite the word *virgin* as opposed to any mention of a *young woman*. Now, I submit that there is a very wide gap between the two descriptions of the female personage in question. A young woman is not necessarily a virgin in the sense of the modern definition. Yet Matthew's fulfillment of Isaiah's so-called prophecy for the Messiah hangs his hat on the fact that Isaiah's *young woman* was the *virgin* Mary.

Matthew's quote of Isaiah's prophecy was literally and factually incorrect. It seems to me that the Christian version of the birth of Jesus has expounded significantly upon Isaiah's comforting prophecy to Ahaz, king of Judah. Isaiah was counseling Ahaz at a time in history when Judah was being besieged by Israel and Syria. This was a prophecy for another time and another place. The Assyrians were a terrible threat to Judah, and King Ahaz needed a bit of encouragement. The Assyrians were a nasty crew, and Ahaz's plight wasn't enviable; Isaiah was trying to give Ahaz comfort that the nation would survive.

Most biblical scholars will agree that for his own reasons, the author of Matthew felt it necessary to embellish and twist the facts surrounding Jesus's ministry so that they fit the many prophecies of the Old Testament concerning the Messiah. Matthew refers to known and unknown prophets, the Psalms, and prophecies made centuries earlier by such men as Jeremiah, Ezekiel, Hosea, Micah, and of course, Isaiah. In doing so, he creates a framework for myth.

The Encyclopedia of Biblical Errancy cites twenty-four alleged references to Messianic prophecies and gives a detailed and scholarly rebuttal as to why each of these more notable passages fails the test of a fulfilled prophecy for the advent of Jesus Christ.[31]

---

31 McKinsey, *The Encyclopedia of Biblical Errancy,* 153–168.

Matthew's virgin birth certainly puts Jesus in the company of several gods and demi-gods such as Adonis, son of the virgin Myrha; Hermes, son of the virgin Maia; Krishna, son of the virgin Devaki; Mani, son of the virgin Meis; Quexalcote, son of the virgin Queen of Heaven; Suchiquecal, etc.

As we examine the life of Jesus of Nazareth, keep in mind that similar claims of virgin births fathered by gods on or around the time of our winter solstice (December 25), infant flight from evil tyrants, forty days of fasting and contemplation, violent deaths, and subsequent bodily resurrection are nothing new to myth, legend, and history. Check out the pre-Christian lives of Mithra, Osiris, Horus, Prometheus, Bacchus, Hermes, Perseus, and several others I fail to list. Of course, these lives are simply the stuff of myth and legends, whereas the life of Christ is "adequately" documented by the New Testament and subsequent church scholarship (which includes some pretty heavy redaction, contradiction, interpolation, and a bit of forgery).

The names of the mothers of several world saviors are derivatives of a root word for water, symbolic of life emerging from a primordial water element: Mary (Miriam in Hebrew), mother of Jesus; Maia, mother of Buddha; Maia, mother of Hermes; Myrrha, mother of Adonis; Mariama, Krishna's mother's title; and others less well-known exist with similar derivatives of the same root word. These "Marys" were centuries prior to Mary, mother of Jesus.

Matthew and his fellow synoptics do a splendid job of confusing the reader of the New Testament with the multiple "Marys" in their respective writings. At one point Matthew lists Mary's (Mary, mother of Jesus) brood as James, Joses, Simon, Judas, and his sisters (being mere women of no consequence to our story, the sisters were naturally left unnamed). Later, Matthew tells us that "Mary, the mother of James and Joses" was among those who witnessed the crucifixion. Yes, she was the mother of James and Joses, but why did the author of Matthew use that choice of words rather than just say, "Mary, the mother of Jesus …"?

John's Gospel (John 19:25), on the other hand, tells us "Now there stood by the cross of Jesus his mother [Mary], and his mother's sister, Mary the wife of Cleophas ..." Mary's sister was named Mary, also? There is a Mary of Bethany, Mary of Magdala, Mary the sister of Lazaras, Luke's unnamed woman at Nairn who anointed Jesus's feet with myrrh, the Mary who sat at Jesus's feet and heard his words, Mark's woman in Bethany who broke open a bottle of nard and anointed Jesus with oil. Some of the unnamed women of the New Testament may have been a Mary; some were not. Is this a deliberate ruse devised by the authors, redactors, interlopers, interlocutors, or other such church figures to diminish the part some of these women played in Jesus's life? If so, what critical information do we fail to learn about the life of Jesus because of their omissions and obfuscation? Or is it simply confusion on the part of the authors who wrote their narratives so many years after Jesus died?

By the time we get through the New Testament, we must begin to wonder if the Christians who penned the Gospels were competing with or copying from the careers of other avatars who met with violent deaths only to rise again. Kersey Graves, in his book subtitled *Christianity before Christ*, gave an interesting accounting of avatars who perished hundreds of years before the time of Christ, listing names and dates and details of their deaths. In many cases these "pagan" saviors were of virgin births, were sacrifices for the atonement of mankind, performed miracles, and preached goodwill and harmony among men.[32]

Of course there is no solid proof that these sixteen crucifixions ever really took place. Stories like these are obviously pagan mythology and should not be confused with the truths and realities of undisputable Christian doctrine. Who could believe such myths?

According to the New Testament, Mary, wife of Joseph, conceived a child and named him Jesus, not Immanuel. If Joseph wasn't the father, then Jesus's claim to Davidic lineage disappears and he could not fulfill any of the Messianic prophecies. None

---

32 Graves, *The World's Sixteen Crucified Saviors,* 102–133.

of the prophecies, however, required birth without human conception. So, to keep things moving along without further digression, let's assume Joseph was the father.

There is considerable confusion as to Jesus's place of birth. The Book of Matthew, which repeatedly attempts to demonstrate that Jesus is the Messiah as prophesied in the Old Testament, has to use a fictitious census to get Joseph and Mary to Bethlehem.[33] The Bible states pretty clearly in several verses that Jesus is from Galilee. Of course, Old Testament scripture can be interpreted to declare that the Christ (Christ or Christos is a Greek translation for the Hebrew title of messiah, or "the anointed") will come from Bethlehem and be a descendant of the house of David. Most Christians accept this as undisputed fact, even though its rather hard to make the case of simultaneous conceptions by both Joseph (to fulfill the Messiah's Davidic genealogy required by prophecy, more precisely, Micah 5:2) as well as the Holy Ghost (to demonstrate Jesus's divinity).

If you read the texts carefully, all versions of the New Testament (John 7:52, John 7:40–42, John 1:45–46, among others) are consistent about Jesus of Nazareth's Galilean origins. The country was a heavily populated kingdom just north of Judah, and of the many towns and villages there, three towns located there are of most interest to this discussion: Capernaum, a fishing community resting on the edge of the Sea of Galilee; Tiberius, Tetrarch Herod Antipas's Hellenized capital city; and Nazareth, resting in the hills to the south not far from the northern border of Judea. So Jesus, the Galilean son of Joseph and Mary, came from the town of Nazareth.

I digress here just for the sake of confusion, I suppose. Nazareth is mentioned nowhere in the Old Testament, the Talmud, nor by the historian Josephus. That doesn't mean it didn't exist, of course. Matthew 2:23 (KJV) refers to an unidentified Old Testament prophecy whereby the Messiah would be called a *Nazarene*. In Judges 13:5 (KJV), a passage concerning Sampson's mother about Sampson states "the child shall be a *Nazarite*

---

33 Harwood, *Mythology's Last Gods*, 258–259.

unto God from the womb: and he shall begin to deliver Israel out of the hand of the Philistines." But this is no prophecy for the Messiah. The word Nazarite means "one who is separate," someone devoted to a spiritual life, like the latter-day Essenes of Jesus's time. Some speculate Jesus was of the Essene sect. Is Matthew using double entendres here? This is the kind of biblical trivia and linguistic confusion that, when taken in the aggregate, starts to undermine the credibility of the entire New Testament.

The Book of Matthew works overtime to show that Jesus is truly the Messiah by fulfilling Jewish prophecy concerning such a "Messiah." Matthew introduces several events that none of the other synoptic gospels mention, such as the astrologers from the East and Herod the Great's (historically unsubstantiated) massacre of the innocents at Bethlehem.

Matthew contrives the Bethlehem birth to show Jesus was born in the City of David as prophesied; his genealogy of Jesus is inaccurate,[34] and it conflicts with Luke's genealogy. According only to the author of Matthew, at the time of Christ's crucifixion, dead people rose and walked the streets of Jerusalem. Matthew becomes so overzealous in his narrative that he would have no credibility to an uninitiated reader who might be reading his work for the first time. Yet the Christian version of Easter relies heavily on the Book of Matthew, and the story is told without apology.

There are a number of parallels between Jesus and Moses as set forth by the author of Matthew: Moses fled from Pharaoh into Midian and stayed until Pharaoh's death, at which time he then returned; Jesus fled from Herod the Great into Egypt and returned only upon the death of Herod. The firstborn of the Egyptians were killed by Moses's god, Yahweh; King Herod massacred all male Hebrew children under the age of two in Bethlehem.

Matthew states in chapter 12:40, that Jesus makes the prophecy, "For Jonah was three days and three nights in the

---

34 Asimov, *Asimov's Guide to the Bible*, 772–778.

whale's belly, so shall the Son of Man be three days and three nights in the heart of the earth." But according to all the Gospels, Jesus was dead Friday evening, all day Saturday, and rose early Sunday morning. This adds up to one full day and two full nights, not the three days and three nights Matthew quotes Jesus as saying. In his zeal to fulfill yet another prophecy, Matthew gets the math wrong.

The author of Mark is somewhat more credible in his narrative. According to Mark, Jesus had four brothers: James, Joses, Simon, and Judas. Matthew and Mark both agree that he also had sisters (Mark 6:3, Matthew 13:56). Mark doesn't make claim to a virgin birth or Davidic genealogies, nor does he expand on events after the crucifixion. He begins his story at the baptism of Jesus by John the Baptist, relates the assembling and identifying of the apostles, and gives a few examples of miracles performed by Jesus. He recounts certain events, keeps it simple, and pretty much lays out the original script for the other gospel writers to follow. There is, however, some confusion as to Mark's account of the ascension, which we'll explore later.

Luke's version of the events pretty much reflects Mark's narrative with a few twists, such as telling us that Mary and Joseph were residents of Nazareth; traveled to Bethlehem for Quirinius's census, where Jesus was born; dropped by Jerusalem for a purification rite; and then returned to Nazareth. Remember Matthew's version of Herod forcing them to flee into Egypt? This contradiction is a serious one for biblical credibility concerning Jesus's birth. Mark skipped all details of Jesus's birth, probably because he knew nothing of it and the subject was not significant to his story, anyway. John's version skips all the virgin birth myth and preempts it by starting out the *Gospel according to Saint John* with his declaration that "In the beginning was the Word … and the Word became flesh and dwelt among us …" John backs this up by declaring that he was sent from God to bear witness that all might believe. John makes no declaration of a virgin birth, no Davidic genealogy, no flight to Egypt, no shepherds and angels. Like Mark, the original gospel narrative, John makes no supernatural claim for the birth of Jesus.

So we are left with the somewhat dubious testament of Matthew and the vague and possibly misleading version told by Luke, who states that the angel Gabriel visited Mary (who was a virgin *at the time of the visit*) and tells her she shall conceive a son and call his name Jesus (not Emmanuel or Immanuel as stated in Matthew's version, but "Jesus"). Gabriel doesn't say or infer that Mary will remain a virgin until Jesus is born. He only is telling her at a time when she was a virgin (whichever definition of "virgin" you may choose to use). Without adding outside commentary to John's narrative or having been influenced by Matthew's version of the events, the reader would simply understand that Gabriel is proclaiming that Mary and Joseph will have a child and that they shall call the child Jesus. Curiously, no immaculate conception is stated by John, Luke, or Mark.

> *Nothing is easier than self-deceit. For what each man wishes, that he also believes to be true.*
> —Demosthenes

The Seven Versions of the Resurrection

*What upsets me is not that you lied to me, but that
from now on I can no longer believe you.*
— Friedrich Wilhelm Nietzsche

Probably more important to the Christian faith than immaculate conception or the Davidic genealogy is the concept of the resurrection and ascension of Jesus. Early Christians accepted the religion before the idea that Jesus was immaculately conceived. Most Gentiles didn't know or care about the requirements that the Messiah had to be from the house of David in Bethlehem. The early Jewish leadership of the church led by Jesus's brother James along with Peter certainly didn't need the miraculous birth or Davidic genealogy to preach Jesus's message to their fellow Jews. James no doubt knew better, anyway.

But both Paul's evangelism to the Gentiles and Peter's preaching to Jews relied on Christ's resurrection and imminent second coming to attract converts. Paul even wrote in 1 Corinthians 15:14, "And if Christ be not risen, then is our preaching vain, and your faith is also vain." All Christian believers (with the possible exception of the Albignesians, who were eventually massacred by the Orthodox Roman Church at the direction of Pope [not so] Innocent III) shared the common belief to some degree or the other that Jesus rose from the grave. Without the miracle of a resurrection, there was no foundation for the church's existence. Christianity couldn't have competed with the various mystery religions, pagan religions, or Orthodox Jewry. Jesus would have been just another failed Jewish prophet who would have passed into anonymity.

The resurrection, when viewed from the uninitiated viewpoint, is an interesting set of contradictions. In the New Testament there are five different accounts of the resurrection of Christ—seven if we count both of Mark's versions and Paul's Letter to the Corinthians. But who's counting?

Matthew tells us that around dawn on Sunday morning, Mary Magdalene and "the other Mary" arrived at the tomb. An earthquake occurred, and an angel of the Lord then rolled away the stone from the door of the tomb, allowing the two Marys to gain entrance into the sepulcher. The guards fell unconscious, and the angel told the two Marys that Christ has risen and that they should go tell the disciples that Jesus went to Galilee before them. The women met Jesus on their way to the disciples, and he told them to tell his brethren that they could see him in Galilee. The disciples went into the mountains of Galilee as Jesus had directed them (when did he give such directions, I wonder?) to worship him. "But some doubted …" Matthew tells us.

Mark's account says that early Sunday morning when the sun had risen, Mary Magdalene, Mary the mother of James, and Salome brought spices to anoint the body. They arrived, finding the large stone already rolled away. They entered the tomb and encountered a young man sitting on the right side (of the tomb?) dressed in a white robe. The young man tells them that they seek Jesus of Nazareth who was crucified, but that Jesus is not there; he has risen. The young man tells them to tell Peter and the disciples that Jesus has gone ahead to Galilee and that they can see him there as he had told them. But the women were afraid, fled the tomb, and said nothing to anyone according to the Revised Standard Version of the New Testament, which ends at chapter 16:8.

However, if we turn to the King James Version, Mark continues on with chapter 16:9, which proceeds to tell us that when Jesus was risen that Sunday, he appeared to Mary Magdalene, out of whom he had cast seven devils. She told the disciples that she had been with him, and they mourned and wept. But they didn't believe her. Later he appeared "in another form" to two of them as they walked in the country. These two also went to the "residue" and told them they had seen Jesus. But they (the disciples) didn't believe them. Finally, Jesus appeared to the eleven during a meal and upbraided them for their lack of belief. He told them to go forth and spread the gospel. After speaking with them, he was received unto Heaven and sat on the right hand of God.

So what's the story here? The Revised Standard Version is significantly different than the King James Version! Same New Testament, same Gospel According to Mark, yet in one version the three women keep silent and the story ends. In the other version, we are told at one point that Mary Magdalene, Mary mother of James, and Salome were the first to visit the tomb early that Sunday morning and left in fear, telling no man of their experience. Yet in the added text starting with verse 9, we are told that Jesus appeared to Mary Magdalene early that day. While this could be a possible scenario, it seems highly unlikely that the three women would go back to the disciples and then Mary Magdalene would repeat the trip and run into Jesus by herself. Since both accounts took place early in the morning, she would have to be moving pretty fast or the disciples were assembled really, really close to the tomb. Maybe this is a clue as to why the Revised Standard Version didn't include the spurious King James addition to its version of Mark.

Luke's account has the women who had come with Joseph of Arimathea from Galilee going to the tomb at early dawn with spices they had prepared. Here they find the stone rolled away from the tomb but no body inside. Two men stood before them reminding them that Jesus had told them he would be crucified and rise on the third day. They remembered the conversation (according to Luke, anyway) and rushed off to tell the eleven apostles. Luke then identifies some of the women in the group as Mary Magdalene, Joanna, Mary the mother of James, and then adds "and the other women." They weren't believed by the apostles. Later, on the road to Emmaus, two of the group met up with Jesus, who joins them in their walk, but they did not recognize him as they walked and discussed the events of the last few days. Finally, during the evening meal to which they had invited the stranger, they recognized their guest as Jesus, at which time he vanished. Later that evening, the women went back to Jerusalem to tell the apostles what they had experienced. Jesus then appeared to the group once again, this time with the apostles apparently present.

John's version of the events has Mary Magdalene going by herself to the tomb before sunrise on Sunday. The stone had already been removed from the entrance to the tomb. She immediately ran to Peter and the unknown disciple "whom Jesus loved" and told them that "They have taken away the Lord out of the sepulcher, and we do not know where they have laid him" (John 20:2, KJV). The two disciples ran to the tomb, entered it, and verified that the body was missing. They believed that someone had taken the body "for as yet they knew not the scripture, that he must rise again from the dead" (John 20:9, KJV). So the two disciples went home, leaving Mary Magdalene alone, weeping at the tomb. Mary then looks inside the tomb and discovers two angels who ask her why she weeps. She answers them and turns around to see Jesus standing there, but fails to recognize him. He asks her why she weeps. Mary, thinking Jesus is the gardener, asks him where he has laid the body so that she may take it away. Jesus then replies, "Mary," at which time she responds, "Teacher." Jesus tells her not to touch him for he has not yet ascended and instructs her to tell his brethren that he is ascending to God. Mary tells the disciples what transpired. That same evening the disciples were visited in a room by Jesus who gave them the Holy Spirit. Thomas expresses doubt. (*Note: This is the same evening that Luke tells us Jesus is dining with the women at Emmaus.)*

Eight days later, again apparently in the same room with the doors and windows shut, Jesus revisits the group. Thomas is among them; Jesus invites him to check out his wounds, at which time Thomas becomes a believer. John tells us Jesus gave the disciples other signs but that these should be enough for the rest of us to believe.

Sometime later, by the Sea of Tiberius, Jesus again reveals himself to the disciples. Some of them were in a boat and saw Jesus on the beach but failed to recognize him. Jesus tells them where to toss the net, and they realize it is Jesus speaking to them. They haul in the fish and are invited by Jesus to join Him at a fire for breakfast. According to the author of John, this was the third time that Jesus had revealed himself to the disciples since he was raised from the dead.

The fifth account of the resurrection is found in Acts 1:3–12. There is no narrative about the tomb. The author of Acts asserts that Jesus presented himself to the apostles over a forty day period before ascending. Jesus told them to wait in Jerusalem until they received the power of the Holy Spirit, and then he ascended. The disciples returned from the mount of Olivet, near Jerusalem, back to the upper room in Jerusalem with Mary the mother of Jesus, the other women, and the brothers of Jesus, where they all prayed.

A sixth recount of Jesus's ascension can be found in 1 Corinthians 15: 4–8. It simply states Jesus died according to the scriptures, he was buried, and he was raised according to scriptures on the third day. He appeared to Cephas, and then to the twelve, and later appeared to over five hundred brethren at one time. Then he appeared to James and then to all the apostles, and finally to Paul of Tarsus, the author of the First Letter of Paul to the Corinthians. Of course, this is the witness of a man who didn't believe any of the Christian gospel at the time it was happening and was a leading persecutor of early

Jewish Christians. *Yet now he bears witness to the very events he earlier ridiculed.*

The point of this exercise is to demonstrate that the witnesses to the resurrection and ascension are at times ambiguous and differ greatly as to what happened. By reading Matthew 28, Mark 16, Luke 24, and John 20–21, Acts 1: 3–14, and 1 Corinthians 15:3–8, anyone can make his or her own assessment as to how reliable the testimony of the Gospels is. Other than Paul's encounter on the road to Damascus as alluded to in Corinthians, none of the narratives are firsthand testimony. And Paul's testament is suspect because in his first life as Saul he was very well aware of the Jewish Christian heresy, yet as Paul he professes to bear witness to the acts and resurrection of Jesus.

The resurrection is the foundation of the Christian faith in its most recent reincarnation. While Christian doctrine has evolved over the centuries and the religion has absorbed or come to terms with many popular customs, pagan and heretical alike, it has never wavered from its doctrine that Jesus Christ was killed by crucifixion and rose from the grave to ascend into Heaven. Some of the details may vary from denomination to denomination, but the death and resurrection are constants. If the resurrection did not occur, Christianity as it is known today could not exist. A fundamental issue in Christianity is having faith in Jesus as God. If the resurrection did not occur, how could a Christian be expected to believe in any of the Gospels? How could one have "faith" when the very hinges of the doors to the church and its doctrine no longer existed?

Actually, while there are those who believe with absolute certainty that Christianity could not exist without the crucifixion and resurrection of Christ, don't believe it. People who have strong beliefs don't lose their faiths that easily. They will not easily accept the fact that they have been led to believe in a supernatural set of circumstances that is fraught with logical fallacies. The true believers will modify their doctrines and rationalize their way out of any problems that might be created from evidence that refutes their beliefs.

The unsophisticated will simply deny that the evidence is valid and continue their beliefs in spite of overwhelming evidence to the contrary. They will attack the source of the information but will not waver in their belief. (Belief that the earth is flat still exists today!) Early Christians believed that the second coming was to occur in their lifetimes as interpreted by Christ's own words. When it failed to materialize, they simply started moving the date forward until finally it was determined that the date of the second coming is not for men to know until it happens.

The more intellectual true believer will adapt the circumstances to fit his or her interpretation of the evidence. For example, if the resurrection was somehow disproved by unimpeachable sources, such a believer might simply contend that the crucifixion and resurrection were symbolic. This believer would accept and agree that Christ's resurrection was not physical, but was actually a spiritual resurrection and ascension. He or she would argue that with or without the crucifixion and resurrection, Jesus Christ's message has not changed. They might even use the various versions of the resurrection found in the New Testament to defend their logic: "The fact there were so many different versions of the events should be obvious testimony that this was meant to be a symbolic event, not an actual historical occurrence. Most of Christ's parables and the recounting of his miracles were allegorical and meant for symbolic use. Some early Christians even debated the divinity of Christ, but they were still all Christians. Nothing has changed." Except the parallax of the true believer. Truth is evasive, even when the facts are well documented. Church doctrine evolves and life goes on. Whatever.

> *Belief in truth begins with doubting all that has hitherto been believed to be true.*
> —Friedrich Wilhelm Nietzsche

A New Testament for the True Believer

A little inaccuracy sometimes saves tons of explanation.

—Saki/Hector Hugh Monro

Each New Testament story of the life of Jesus is told secondhand or thirdhand. There are no primary sources. Unlike the public crucifixion, there is no public ascension. It was revealed only to the brethren of the church, who tell us we must believe all this or burn in Hell. Only through faith can the Christian's soul be saved. Good works and a clean life without believing in Christ don't really count toward heavenly credit.

The New Testament has many stories of the acts and miracles performed by Jesus, his parables, and his frequent use of allegory and hidden meanings. These have all been examined by scholars and Christian apologists, and I shall not spend time trying to analyze and prove the unprovable. The debates will rage on until the second coming. The texts of the New Testament were compiled after the Roman–Jewish War and the destruction of the temple in 70 CE. All the original players in Christ's drama were by then dead, Saul of Tarsus was dead, and the Gospels were being anonymously compiled and edited by the Gentile Christians living under Roman rule. The center of the church had by now shifted from Jerusalem to Rome.

Whether you believe or don't believe the stories of the New Testament is of no consequence to me. If you are a Christian, I only ask you to at least think about *why* you believe what you believe and the sources for your beliefs. After countless translations, redactions, and changes in the original texts, how accurate is the text of New Testament?

We have the Jewish Torah and Hebrew texts to keep the Christian scribes honest with the Old Testament. The New Testament is an anonymous assembly of selected Christian texts from a huge selection available.[35] That selection was narrowed over the centuries as certain texts found popularity with various early Christian sects. Over time these texts spread throughout the Christian world as some fell from favor and others began to enjoy common usage.

Everyone prefers belief to the exercise of judgment.
—Seneca

---

35 Mack, *Who Wrote the New Testament?*, 6–7.

Biblical Errancies of the New Testament

The Bible may be the truth, but it is not the whole truth and nothing but the truth.

—Samuel Butler

There are many, many contradictions, forgeries, inaccuracies, and biblical facts that do not correspond to historical sources. It is not my mission here to point out each and every biblical error, forgery, or fallacy. There are entirely too many for me to name and then to have to provide documentation of. Books have been written on this topic, so I shall not attempt to take us very far down that path. I simply wish to make the reader aware of the suspicion one should have concerning taking the New Testament as the gospel truth. I'll cite just a few, leave critical thinking to those who can, and we'll move on.

Herod ascended the throne of Judah in 37 BCE; he died in 4 BCE. For Jesus to have been born "in the days of Herod the King," as stated in the New Testament, he had to have been born four years "before Christ."[36] During Jesus's lifetime, Galilee was ruled by tetrarch Herod Antipas, son of Herod the Great (who had ruled Judah at the time of Jesus's birth).

The Messianic Prophecies are outlined in various studies of Christianity, citing verses from the Old Testament Bible and

---

36 Asimov, *Asimov's Guide to the Bible*, 787.

Jewish scriptures. There are dozens of verses that have been construed as to prophecy and its fulfillment by the life and death of Jesus of Nazareth. Prophecies left unfulfilled are to be addressed in Christ's second coming. However, the Jewish Bible does not prophesy a "second coming"; this is a Christian device to deal with the fact that according to Jewish traditions and messianic prophecies, when the "Messiah" (the Anointed One) comes to fulfill that which was written in the Law of Moses and in the Prophets, the results will be a millennium of universal peace, etc. We all know *that* didn't happen, don't we? No sequel is required in the Jewish version of the messianic prophecy. Any messiah that fulfills the prophecies as written wouldn't have to come back a second time to finish the job. The Christians have taken Jewish prophecy and adapted selective parts of it in an attempt to "prove" that Christ was the true Messiah.

To illustrate just a few of the major prophecies and the issues surrounding their fulfillment, I submit the following:

Isaiah the prophet is noted by Christians for his predictions of the messiah by those who choose to interpret his words as such. Isaiah 7:14 says, "the young woman is with child and shall bear a son and shall call his name Immanuel" (NRSV). Our old buddy Matthew writes in Matthew 1:17–18 about genealogy and prophecy by putting Isaiah's words into the mouth of the angel of the Lord who says, "Look, the virgin shall conceive and bear a son, and they shall name him Emmanuel." Mary named her child Joshua, or in Greek, "Jesus." Who, then, is Emmanuel?

One problem with this "prophecy" is that when Isaiah was speaking, he was speaking directly to King Ahaz to lift his spirits when Ahaz had heard that the dreaded Assyrians and their allies were uniting against him. Isaiah was telling Ahaz that the Lord would give Ahaz a sign that by the time the child mentioned in the prophecy learned right from wrong, the two allied kingdoms threatening Judah will be deserted. He says nothing of a promised messiah whose name would be Immanuel.

Isaiah 52:13 through 53:12 are noted for their messianic prophecies by Christians and probably contain the most important verses of prophecy concerning Christ.[37] When combined, the verses set forth a series of predictions that have traditionally been applied by Christians as prophecy that has been fulfilled by Christ. The "prophecies" can all be refuted by an aggressive critic or defended by the true believer, but to an objective reader, Isaiah's story is about a despised, deformed, mute, suffering servant of the Lord who endures oppression, infirmary, and an ignoble death and burial only to praised for remaining righteous through his ordeals in life.

Isaiah 52:13 says that the Lord's suffering servant shall prosper and be exalted, lifted, and shall be very high. (Did Jesus prosper and was he lifted to a high station in life?) Isaiah 53:10 states he shall see his offspring and prolong his days. (Did Jesus have offspring?) Isaiah 53:12 says he will divide the spoil with the strong. (Was Jesus involved with any division of spoils or riches?) Was Jesus "smitten by God," deformed, and oppressed? The entire passage in Isaiah moves between past and future tense, some of which implies that the servant has or is undergoing his ordeal in life during the time of Isaiah's interlocution. The descriptions of the servant and harshness of his life do not resemble anything near the New Testament's portrait of Jesus Christ.

Pauline Christianity is founded on the precept that one cannot find salvation and go to Heaven unless he or she believes in Jesus Christ (John 3:36, John 3:18, 1 John 5:12). Christian doctrine, stripped of all other tenets surrounding the issue, is that faith is the sole ticket to enter the gates of Heaven. Matthew 19:16–18 quotes Jesus as saying, "if you wish to enter into life, keep the commandments." James 2:14–24 tells us that "faith by itself, if it has no works, is dead." And later, "You see that a person is justified by works and not faith alone." So, which is it? Do we find salvation through faith, works, both, or neither?

Luke 3:23 gives us Jesus's genealogy going back seventy-five generations to Adam using Joseph, son of Heli, as the genealogical bloodline. With the small error of counting Cainan twice (see the

---

37 McKinsey, *The Encyclopedia of Biblical Errancy*, 160–163.

genealogy in Genesis, which is nineteen generations from Adam to Abraham instead of Luke's twenty), Luke is consistent with the biblical genealogy. Going forward in time from Abraham, Luke's genealogy matches that of Matthew's from Abraham to David. He then picks up the descent from David through one of David's sons named Nathan whereas Matthew tells us the descent goes from David to Solomon and on through the line of Judean kings. The two genealogies meet again at Joseph (husband to Mary, mother of Jesus) but fail to agree on the name of Joseph's father. Matthew gives Joseph's father's name as Jacob, whereas Luke gives us Heli. Matthew lists forty-two generations from Jesus back to Abraham; Luke lists fifty-five.[38] And Mary, a Levite, was a virgin who, according to Christian doctrine, conceived not from Joseph, but from the Holy Ghost. So how does Jesus's genealogy meet the messianic requirement that he be of the Davidic bloodline?

We have already addressed the discrepancies in the birth and resurrection of Jesus, so those items do not need to be revisited. I concede that any testament from several sources will undoubtedly have discrepancies. People tell the same story in different ways, omitting important facts and often get minor facts wrong. So the New Testament is entitled to some variations and contradictions. But to call this very selective and redacted collection of testaments "the word of God" stretches the imagination and diminishes the concept of an omnipotent being.

The benchmarks and original sources of the New Testament consist of various scrolls from various sects that have been worked and reworked, ending up in what is known as the New Testament. The canon known today as the New Testament is from these texts, based on the political and theological choices of (according to Eusebius of Caesarea) "more than 250" (mostly Greek) Bishops congregating at the Council of Nicea in 325 CE under the supervision of Roman emperor Constantine.[39] With

---

38 Asimov, *Asimov's Guide to the Bible*, 937–940.
39 Chadwick, *The Early Church*, 130.

apologies to Otto Von Bismark on his remark concerning the making of laws and sausage, I submit that if true believers really knew how the New Testament was put together, they wouldn't be eating pork today.

Organized Christianity has probably done more to retard the ideals that were its founders' than any other agency in the world.

—Richard Le Gallienne

The Evolution of Christianity

The careful reader of the New Testament will find three Christs described: One who wished to preserve Judaism, one who wished to reform it, and one who built a system of his own.
—Robert G. Ingersoll

As stated earlier, the New Testament was compiled sometime after the destruction of the temple in Jerusalem and the end of the Roman–Jewish War. The evangelist Paul (formerly known as Saul of Tarsus) had left a body of written works outlining his version of Christianity and laid the foundation for most of Christianity's current doctrine. It was not the doctrine of the original Jerusalem church led by James, the brother of Jesus, who continued to maintain Jewish tradition.

Paul had quarreled with the Jerusalem church leaders, Peter and Jesus's brother James, about the idea of requiring Gentile converts to be circumcised as well as about other issues. Paul continued to preach and correspond with many of the Gentile Christian communities. He was known to preach doctrine that was not approved by the Jerusalem church, which still followed Jewish custom and ceremony. Paul's teachings frequently and significantly contradicted what the Synoptic Gospels tell us were

Jesus's words.[40] A major rift developed between Paul and the Jerusalem church because of Paul's pronounced abandonment of the Torah, his teachings being contrary to James's instructions about what should be taught to Gentile believers, and his theology of salvation through faith.

Around AD 62, James, the brother of Jesus, was condemned by the Jewish high priest Ananus for heresy and stoned to death in Jerusalem. Jesus's family, the desposynoi, continued to control the Jerusalem church for several years thereafter.[41] Their followers were known at that time as the Nazarenes and later known as Ebionites. They believed that Jesus was a human being of natural birth, continued to follow the Torah, and that Jesus's original teachings were profaned and polluted by Paul.[42]

After the destruction of the temple in AD 70, the Jewish Christians, along with other Jews, were dispersed by the Romans to such places as Caesarea, Alexandria, Egypt, and similar locations within the empire. Broken and leaderless, the Ebionite church went into decline, and the message that Jesus had been trying to convey to his Jewish brethren was corrupted by Paul and passed on to the Gentile Christians in the form of Pauline Christianity.

While James's martyrdom in AD 62 is well documented, the fates of Peter and Paul are not so clear. Peter, according to Eusebius and Origen, went to Rome as an old man and was martyred by crucifixion during the reign of Nero around AD 64. Other than the word of these two church historians, we have no documentation or collaboration of Peter's end.

Eusebius's version of Paul's demise is that he returned to Rome and was executed in AD 67. No one is certain whether Paul was condemned and executed during his arrest in Rome or if he went to Spain and died a natural death. The Book of Acts doesn't tell us, and Paul's fate is left to the imagination.

---

40 McKinsey, *The Encyclopedia of Biblical Errancy*, 427–435.
41 Grant, *Saint Peter*, 141–142.
42 Maccoby, *The Mythmaker*, 174–176.

In any case, after the destruction of the temple in Jerusalem by the Romans, Pauline Christianity survived, headquartered first in Antioch and then later in Rome. By the time of the Jewish Bar Kochba insurrection against the Romans in 135 CE, the gulf between Christians and Jews had become complete. Christians had abandoned the Torah and attributed new meanings to Jewish Scriptures and customs. Passover evolved into Easter, the Sabbath became Sunday, circumcision was no longer a requirement for the faithful, and beliefs that had originally been minor Jewish heresies became Hellenized, distorted, and appropriated by Gentiles to form the basis of Christianity as we now know it.

James, brother of Jesus, and his small group of early Christians fell into obscurity, overwhelmed by Pauline Christianity. Church history doesn't even concern itself with the fate of these Ebionites who withdrew from Jerusalem in 66 CE and moved across the Jordan River to Pella at the start of the Jewish War with Rome. The Ebionites were persecuted by the Jewish Sanhedrin and considered outcasts. They were also persecuted by the Pauline Christians. It is irony that the very first Christians, friends and relatives of Jesus, were destined to become some of the first to be called heretics by the Christian Church.[43]

In the year 325 CE, Emperor Constantine established Christianity as an official state religion, donated properties to the church, helped promote its doctrines, and even allowed certain "pagan" temples to be converted to holy Christian shrines. From this point forward, until the Reformation by Martin Luther in 1517, Christianity became institutionalized under the doctrine and dogma of the Roman Catholic Church. Any deviation from church doctrine was considered heresy and subject to severe repercussions.

During these years, the Holy Catholic Church brought us such heavenly events as the eight Crusades to the Holy Land between 1096 CE and 1270 CE, which brought indiscriminate killing of Jews, Christians, and Muslims to the people living in

---

43 Wilson, *Jesus-A Life*, 248–249.

the paths of the Crusaders. It brought us the Congregation of the Inquisition, which maimed, burned, and confiscated the properties of accused heretics across Europe from around 1230 CE to 1908 CE, at which time the term "Inquisition" was dropped from the Holy Office's label and since 1965 has been known officially as "The Sacred Congregation for the Doctrine of the Faith."

The church sponsored the eradication of the Albigensians, including the slaughter of over twenty thousand Cathars and Christians—men, women, and children alike—at Beziers during the thirty year long papal war against the heretical Cathars in southern France. Papal power was behind the 1572 St. Bartholomew's massacre of ten thousand Protestants in France and similar atrocities during the Reformation. Religion (superstition) was the basis of accusations of devil worshiping and witch hunts by both Protestants and Catholics, which resulted in the burning, hanging, or torturing of countless innocent women. The church extended its reach into the New World by forcing native conversion to Christianity in the Portuguese and Spanish territories—including California, South America, and the Caribbean—through torture, rape, and enslavement. [44]

The list of church atrocities is much too long to detail in this discussion. Books are available to those who are curious as to the dark history of Christianity. The apologist will simply say that the church has changed enormously since those days. I answer that during my aeons of existence, man's nature has yet to change. He corrupts any institution or organization that he has ever created. Sooner or later, unless somehow restricted, man tends toward excess. And as noted earlier, excessive religious zeal is very dangerous, especially in the hands of a person who has access to economic or political power.

So there you have it. Christianity with its warts. I find it amusing to hear all the problems of the world attributed to "the devil," when history records most of our problems have originated from organized religions. Christians fight Muslims

---

44 Ellerbe, *The Dark Side of Christian History*, 74, 81–92, 95, 136–138.

and persecute Jews, Hindus fight Buddhists and Muslims, Jews fight Muslims, Muslims fight everybody, and yet they all want to blame me for the woes of the world.

> *At least I know, no matter which religion is right,*
> *when I die, I'm going straight to Hell.*
> —Adam Tilove

Major Cults Evolving into Mainstream Religion

The greater the ignorance, the greater the dogmatism.

—Sir William Osler

Most true believers have confined their searches for salvation to the major religions previously discussed. The major religions have stood the test of time and have garnered their respective shares of the human population. Some continue to grow their market share, while others have entered a period of decline or, at best, maintain their share of earthly souls. These theologies have achieved respectability in the market for the hearts and minds of man. There are many minor theologies that will remain unexplored because they are too many and too small to take the time to dwell upon. And many are simply minor variations of one or more of the major religions.

However, no self-respecting demon from Hell would fail to mention a couple of growing franchises in the soul business. These cults have reached critical mass (pun intended) and are now accepted by many as legitimate religions. They were created during a period when the printing press was available and documentation was reasonably permanent at the time the doctrine was evolving. Yet they, too, seem to be omitting, changing, or contradicting previously published material facts, mixing truth with myth and legend over time. As time creeps forward and new generations take up the call to believe, verifiable facts will fall into oblivion and legend will prevail, just as it has in the major religions. The official records tend to change or become lost over the decades and centuries as the religion evolves. It is a sad but interesting phenomenon to observe.

It is fascinating yet troublesome to observe otherwise intelligent people becoming assimilated body and soul into organizations that (to the objective mind) are obviously designed to create codependent followers to become the base of power for the organization and its ruling elite. Sometimes these organizations are called "cults"; often they are known by other definitions that disguise their true nature. Whatever the name, these organizations build their power on the foundation of a mass of marching morons they have brainwashed and converted into fanatical true believers. Obviously, intelligence does not equal common sense nor does it ensure emotional independence. Some of the recruited souls eventually escape from the orbit of these psychological black holes, others remain and are absorbed into the entity, and the rest are destroyed.

> You think that, if you call imprisonment "true freedom," people will be attracted to the prison. And the worst of it is you're quite right.
> —Aldous Huxley, *Eyeless in Gaza*

The Church of Jesus Christ
of Latter-Day Saints

Some revelations are of God; some revelations are of man; and some revelations are of the devil.
—Joseph Smith Jr.

A man named Joseph Smith II was born in Sharon, Vermont, on December 23, 1805. By age ten, he moved with his family to Palmyra, New York, which was then a bustling town with a population of around four thousand. Here, in part of what was known as the "burnt over" district (due to the many religious revivals passing through that "burnt the religious enthusiasm out the inhabitants" because of their frequency and intensity), Joseph spent his boyhood and was exposed to various religious doctrines and fervor. Religious eccentricity was so common that it became the norm during this period of evangelism and religious experimentation. By now the family was relatively poor, having exhausted Joseph's mother's dowry and proving unsuccessful as farmers. Joseph grew up knowing debt, poverty, and hard labor on the farm.

Joe's adolescence and early adulthood was spent treasure hunting, digging for money through the use of spells and incantations, divining, and seer stones. He experienced a brush or two with the law as the result of some of his money-digging activities, but his reputation among some of his neighbors was more that of a rogue than that of a felon. Joseph even admitted to the fact that he harbored some unsavory conduct in his past.[45]

When he was twenty-one, his spiritualism changed from necromancy and money digging to becoming the recipient of a revelation from God and the founder of a new cult religion, one of many that had sprung up in the area during this period. Joe proclaimed himself a prophet. Joseph later received considerable bad press from the local Palmyra newspapers, but at the time, his claim to revelations from God pretty much went unnoticed except for those few family and believers who accepted his belated revelation of his dreams and visions as gospel.

From here, facts become disputed and sometimes contradictory. According to Joseph, his ministry began around 1820 at the age of 14. This is doubtful since in 1826 Joe was still doing money digging for hire and was accused of disorderly conduct and being an imposter. He stood trial and was pronounced guilty. The resulting sentence is buried in history with the money he was supposed to locate and dig up. Later he had a couple of other trials, but was found not guilty.[46]

During this time, Joe fell in love with Emma Hale, daughter of Isaac Hale, who thought him nothing more than a scoundrel and imposter. In spite of her father's objections, Joe covertly arranged a marriage to Emma and the deed was done in 1827. During the next five years of his life, Joe Smith put together the foundation of what is now the Church of Jesus Christ of Latter-Day Saints, also known as the Mormons.

In June 1827, he told his father a story of a spirit telling him about some golden plates buried near their home, guarded by a toad. When Joe had tried to retrieve the plates years earlier, the toad was transformed into a man who hit him and would not let him retrieve the plates. Later, in September 1827, Joe confided

---

45 Brodie, *No Man Knows My History*, 17.
46 Ibid., 30–32.

in his father that he was now authorized to dig up and translate the golden plates. He claimed that in 1823 he had been visited by a messenger of God named Moroni who told him of the book containing the everlasting gospel, written upon gold plates that were buried along with a breastplate and two seer stones, called Urim and Thummim, which would allow him to translate the plates. For four years he visited the site annually, and he was finally allowed to retrieve the plates in the fall of 1827. Joseph warned his family that it meant instant death to anyone other than himself to look upon the plates.

Joe enlisted Emma to take down his dictation of the translation of the plates, since he hadn't learned to write. The plates told the story through the words of Nephi, a Hebrew who had left Jerusalem in 600 BCE along with his father, Lehi, their families, and other followers. They sailed to America and, over time, divided into the peaceable, religiously faithful white race of Nephites and the idolatrous, bloodthirsty red race of Lamanites. Thus, according to Joe Smith's translation of the plates, the native Amerindians were the descendants of those Hebrews who came to the continent in 600 BCE. This is the same theory pushed by a Vermont church pastor named Ethan Smith, who published *A View of the Hebrews* (or *The Ten Tribes of Israel in America*) in 1823.

Parallels between Joe's translation of the plates into the Book of Mormon and Ethan Smith's poorly researched book, *A View of the Hebrews*, are material and significant, suggesting major plagiarism on Joe's part. A reading of David Persuitte's book, *Joseph Smith and the Origins of the Book of Mormon* (McFarland & Co., Jefferson, NC, 1985) lays out several pages of comparisons between Ethan Smith's novel and Joseph Smith's "translation" of the Book of Mormon. The Book of Mormon was translated as King James English when neither such language nor dialect existed at the time the plates were supposedly created. The fact that Joseph Smith's Nephite prophets quote from Isaiah creates another strange anomaly for the true believer. There is also the issue of nearly identical texts written down by Lucy

Smith, Joe's mother, of dreams that Joseph Sr. had. Joseph Sr.'s dreams can be found duplicated in the Book of Mormon under a chapter entitled *The Vision of Lehi*.[47] Details involving the Urim and Thummim, the breastplate, and treasure cave are right out of Masonic lore. Such questionable details as these should give one pause as to the supposed divinity of the Book of Mormon.

In any case, Joe found a patron, Martin Harris, willing to finance his translation of the plates, which were written in what Joe called "reformed Egyptian hieroglyphics." Harris took over the task of taking down Joe's dictation. Between the two of them, they churned out enough prose to bring the total, including what Emma had transcribed, to 116 pages. Harris eventually took the 116 pages back to his farm to show his wife, Lucy. Lucy, who feared that Martin would be bilked out of what modest assets they owned by mortgaging their farm to finance the publication of the Book of Mormon, stole and hid the 116 pages. She defied Joseph to reproduce the translation, since he had claimed it was a divine message and should be easily transcribed again from the plates he claimed to hold.

Joe was counting on profits from the book to help his father avoid foreclosure of the farm as well as to produce income for him and Emma. Joe's prayers were answered by a divine dictate to use a smaller set of plates called the plates of Nephi, and only after they were translated would he go back to the original plates and begin the translation from page 117 where he had left off. The plates of Nephi, it was revealed, were an alternate version of the stolen version, which would not be retranslated. (Later, still another set of 24 plates would surface to cover the Jaredites who came to America around 2,500 BCE after fleeing the Tower of Babel fiasco.)

A schoolteacher from Palmyra, New York, named Oliver Cowdery took up the dictation, and in three months they had completed a manuscript of approximately 275,000 words. Martin Harris mortgaged his farm and ultimately paid the $3,000.00 required to print 5,000 copies of the Book of Mormon, alias

---

47 Brodie, *No Man Knows My History*, 58.

the Golden Bible. The result of all this was an amalgam of the King James Version of the books of Isaiah, Matthew, John, and Revelations[48] mixed with a novelized story based on Ethan Smith's book, *A View of the Hebrews*, and a touch of Masonic mysticism. Later would come the Book of Enoch, the Book of Moses, The Pearl of Great Price, and Doctrines and Covenants.

As the Book of Mormon was being published, Joe Smith moved on to organizing his church. He was no longer the good ole "Joe Smith" his friends and acquaintances had known him as. He gave himself a title: Joseph Smith, Seer, Translator, Prophet, Apostle of Jesus Christ, and Elder of the Church through the will of God the father, and the grace of your Lord Jesus Christ.[49] He also assumed the biblical name Enoch when it suited him. The autocratic Church of Christ was up and running. In 1834, the church was renamed the Church of Latter-Day Saints. In 1838, Joe had another revelation, and the church was renamed The Church of Jesus Christ of the Latter-Day Saints. Most know its practitioners as Mormons, after the reputed author of the Book of Mormon, whose testimony was delivered to the prophet Joseph Smith in the form of golden plates by Mormon's son, Moroni.

Hundreds of books have been written on the history of Joseph Smith and his ministry, so we shall not dwell on the minutia and many questionable issues that are a part of Joe's history and character. Though uneducated and unable to write, the man had hubris and was imaginative. His detractors will outline the many contradictions in his stories of visions, golden plates from God, the authorship of the Book of Mormon, polygamy (some with women still married to other men, and in direct violation of verses in the Book of Mormon and the Doctrines and Covenants condemning such practices), failed prophecies, Masonic rites woven into church temple rites, Mormon militia, and his dreams of empire and confrontations with the United States government, charges of treason, and all

---

48 Brodie, *No Man Knows My History*, 57.
49 Ibid., 84.

the other fascinating elements of Mormon history that occurred during Joseph's lifetime.

As he gained stature and power, he revised his own history to improve his image as prophet and founder of the church. To understand the character of the founder and self-proclaimed prophet is to better understand the genesis of the theology he created and the cult of worship that has evolved after his passing. Joseph Smith died in jail, murdered by an angry mob (the Warsaw militia and the Carthage Greys) in Carthage, Missouri, on June 27, 1844. The Mormon theocracy Joseph Smith was trying to create came to an inglorious end, but his church survived under the auspices of Brigham Young, who moved the Mormons to what is now the "church state" of Utah, which they control through a de facto theocracy.

The Church of Jesus Christ of Latter-Day Saints (LDS) believes that Joseph Smith is the prophet who restored the priesthood and reestablished the church of Jesus Christ, and that divine truths come from God through revelations to apostles and prophets. They believe in plural gods—that the Father, Son, and Holy Ghost are each separate and distinct gods who form the Godhead—and that man can become a god through exaltation. God, according to LDS theology as preached by Joseph Smith, was once a man who has now become exalted. This contradicts both Old and New Testament theology. Mormons accept the Bible but qualify their acceptance to only those portions that are translated correctly. They also believe that the Book of Mormon is the word of God. (Joe and I both get a kick out of that one!)

The theology of the Latter-Day Saints professes to be Christian in nature, but any fundamental Christian believer will take exception to LDS doctrine when it is more closely examined. Just like Christianity hijacked Judaic beliefs and monotheism and reworked the theology, Joseph Smith was doing the same to Christianity, creeping toward polytheism and revealing the existence of a Heavenly Mother who is the wife of God in Heaven.[50] Had he lived, there is little doubt he

50   Robert, *Mormonism Unmasked*, 52–53.

would have rewritten the entire Old Testament and possibly the New Testament also. The doctrines of the Latter-Day Saints hide behind the image of Jesus Christ, but it is centered upon the theology created by Joseph Smith.

LDS theology does not meet the common definition of Christianity, even though most Mormons consider themselves Christians. As a matter of fact, they believe that they are the only true faith that will be allowed eternal salvation. That means all you Gentiles (non-Mormons) will be needing reservations for Hell. I'll be waiting.

> As soon as one's convictions become unshakeable, evidence ceases to be relevant—except as a means to convert the unbelievers. Factual inaccuracies … are excusable in light of the Higher Truth.
> —P. H. Hoebens

Scientology

None are more hopelessly enslaved than those who falsely believe they are free.
                                —Johann Wolfgang von Goethe

Scientology is a "religion" created by a man named Lafayette Ron Hubbard. Like Mohammed, Joseph Smith, and other great creators of religions, Ron was a bigamist for a brief period in his life.[51] Hubbard was a prolific science fiction writer who was best known in the fifties for writing a popular book called *Dianetics: The Modern Science of Mental Health*. Dianetics was a process of psychotherapy L. Ron Hubbard put together from the works of philosophers and scientific minds like Alfred Korzybski, Sigmund Freud, Vance Packard, Fodor, Rank, and others who were involved with the human mind, spirit, and psychology.[52]

While controversial, Dianetics has its adherents and may have been beneficial to a number of people at some point in its evolvement. It is a form of self-analysis using another person called the "auditor" to work the "patient" through his or her unconscious traumas. The success of Dianetics lay in its ability to

---

51 Atack, *A Piece of Blue Sky, Scientology, Dianetics and L. Ron Hubbard Exposed*, 101.
52 Ibid., 122, 370, 374.

locate and clear recorded traumas in the unconscious memory of the individual.

Hubbard claimed that the conscious mind is the "analytical mind," whereas the unconscious mind, the "reactive mind," operates at an imbecile level and cannot operate rationally. Certain traumas are caused by incidents implanted and recorded by the reactive mind, which creates an irrational response mechanism in the individual. That response mechanism manifested itself in sickness, depression, or other negative traits acquired by the individual. Dianetics, through its auditing process, would "clear" the individual from these mnemes, which Hubbard called "engrams." This is known in psychiatric circles as abreaction. People undergoing Dianetic treatment were called "preclears." Once they had received the proper auditing and all engrams were identified and erased, they would then be "clear."

After a while, the novelty of Dianetics wore off, and the public's attention turned to other things. Hubbard's fertile imagination and genius for acquiring and popularizing subjects of general interest moved him to take the Dianetics concept and turn it into a religion. Having been deeply influenced by Aleister Crowley and his brand of mysticism he called "magick," Hubbard created a complete cosmology and theology with axioms, core beliefs, and rituals. This belief system is a mixture of pseudoscience, psychotherapy, franchising, and religion sprinkled with traits of Catholicism, fascism, and science fiction. While Nietzsche wrote of the Will to Power, Hubbard succeeded in actualizing it through Scientology. The Dianetic clinics were turned into commercial religious franchises for Scientology, and in 1954 the First Church of Scientology was formed. By becoming a church, Hubbard would foil the efforts of the American Medical Association and the IRS. Religious beliefs generally transcend medical authority, and churches are usually granted tax-free status for their nonbusiness activities. [53]

---

53 Corydon, *L. Ron Hubbard: Messiah or Madman?*, 330–334.

The story of L. Ron Hubbard's life and adventures as he gave it was quite colorful and amazing. The factual story of Hubbard's life is just as fascinating but is much darker than the sanitized versions put out by Scientologist literature. He was married three times. Hubbard spent years as a reclusive self-professed naval commodore, commanding his religious empire through a fascistlike group he called the "Sea Organization." He knew how to use the legal system through his doctrine of "fair game" to harass and ruthlessly destroy perceived and real threats to his authority over those who would follow him. He was a prolific writer, penning over twenty books, including *The Brainwashing Manual*, *Science of Survival*, *Scientology: A History of Man*, *Scientology: The Fundamentals of Thought*, and others related to the business and religion of psychotherapy as practiced by Scientologists.

The cosmology of Scientology goes back seventy million years ago, when an evil being called Xenu was president of the Galactic Confederation. Earth, at that time called Teegeeack, was one of the seventy-six planets that comprised the overpopulated confederation. Xenu ordered the excess population to be sent to Teegeeack (a.k.a. Earth), where these people were destroyed by nuclear explosions. Their spirits, called thetans, were subsequently implanted with religious and technological images and data, which they retained over the eons. According to Hubbard's theology, human beings are comprised of clusters of these tortured souls, called body thetans.

According to Scientology doctrine, a thetan governs the individual at the conscious level whereas the body and its low-grade spirit or soul is controlled by what is known as a "genetic entity," which apparently moves on to another body after the body dies. The thetan is the actual personality of the individual.[54] Hubbard's manual, *Scientology: A History of Man*, previously called *What to Audit*, covers much of this topic, which is the foundation of Scientology doctrine and practice.

---

54 Atack, *A Piece of Blue Sky, Scientology, Dianetics and L. Ron Hubbard Exposed*, 131–134.

The warrior religions would simply know thetans to be the equivalent of demons, angels, or agents of Satan, depending upon their theological proclivities at the time. Hubbard has updated the concept of demons and has tried to give the concept scientific cover. Junk science and science fiction, however, are not valid substitutes for verifiable scientific knowledge. By wrapping Dianetics and Scientology in the cloak of "religion," L. Ron Hubbard has moved his ideas from the realm of science—with its demands for postulates, hypothesis, and proofs—to the unprovable world of religious belief. Well done, Ron.

Scientologists believe in reincarnation and past and future lives, thus the thetan-beings with their various implants continue to inhabit man's psyche and are the individual human spirit that makes up the essence of human beings. Operating thetans (OTs) are immortal and can function without a physical body. They have the ability to perform such feats as telepathy, telekinesis, levitation, spiritual movement through time and space, and the power to will events to happen.

Once a Scientologist has been "cleared," he is ready to move on to the next level of improvement. This level of training must be done at the organizational level (church org) because the mission or field office cannot conduct audits past the level of "clear." There are several levels of OT training, secret "tech" training, and elitist levels to which the advanced Scientologist aspires.

Buried in all this psychotheology are layers of awareness that the Scientologist only learns when he or she reaches certain levels within the organization. The church promotes and controls various front groups and affiliates, which may or may not be publically linked to Scientology. Such groups include the Citizens' Commission on Human rights; Narconon; United Churches; Dianetics; Foundation for Advancements in Science and Education; Church of Spiritual Technology; Author Services, Inc.; and a host of others.[55] The church advertises with slick promotional ads on late night television, inviting respondents

---

55 Corydon, *L. Ron Hubbard: Messiah or Madman?*, 452–454.

to learn how to achieve a better life. They use public figures and celebrities to legitimize their organization and proselytize potential members. They have Internet sites under various entities, which link to Scientology. Their public relations are first class, seemingly pure and innocent, and very convincing. This is the bait used to attract the unsuspecting and vulnerable, called "raw meat" by Hubbard and his Rondroids.[56]

As the newly recruited, preclear Scientologist begins his or her training, subtle changes in meanings and vocabulary begin to take place. The altruistic attitude of the church changes slightly to reflect the fact that humans who are not practicing Scientology are "wogs." (Wog is a derogatory term used by Scientologists to describe the rest of humanity. A wog is a humanoid too stupid to realize the good that is being done by Scientology.) The newly converted Scientologist is taught that only through recruitment into the church can those people be helped. Deception, lies, and dishonest behavior are acceptable so long as the actions help the church in its goal to survive and expand. Since Scientologists believe that they are the ones who will survive the cataclysm that will eventually come upon the world, the end justifies the means. Any such deceit is deemed pardonable by the church because it is for the greater good that some individual sacrifices must be made.

By this point, the new Scientologist has spent a considerable sum of his savings for training. He has been given the hard sell and probably exhausted his financial resources for training and certification. He is pretty much hooked. He knows all the acronyms, buzz words, and terminology. He has learned the Axioms, the Logics, the Prelogics, and the Factors. He has learned and practiced the Auditor's Code and the Code of the Scientologist. Scientology is helping him work out all his problems and identify his past-life traumas. He has completed his training routines and has confessed all his dark thoughts, relationship issues, and personal problems through the audit

---

56 Atack, *A Piece of Blue Sky, Scientology, Dianetics and L. Ron Hubbard Exposed*, 336.

process. His file holds the residue of everything he ever said, did, or thought that needed to be processed. He is now a certified auditor and can audit others for cash remuneration.

As he moves into the higher levels of the organization, the Scientologist "knows" that what he has been taught is the truth. He "knows" it works. The only time someone hasn't benefitted from Scientology training is because they were subversive, "out-ethics," or possibly an SP (suppressive person, a person with evil intentions). To a Scientologist, the process is unimpeachable, so any failure must be the fault of the preclear being audited.

The practiced Scientologist is firm in his belief. He is now supremely confident in what he "knows" and is ready to move to a higher level where he may begin his quest for "total freedom." His human level problems have been cleared, and he is ready to begin org training for the secretive OT levels only alluded to during his early training. His training has developed his confidence level and his knowledge to the point that he *knows* he is superior to the wog pool from which he came. From this point on, the concept of total freedom becomes an oxymoron, because the grip of the church becomes oppressive and tyrannical.

The Sea Org staff and administrators represent the more hard-core individuals of the church. They have all taken the levels of training necessary to become trusted and knowledgeable Scientologists. They are dedicated to the cause and work for very little pay. They are convinced in the nobility of what they do. It is during this phase of one's Scientology experience that persuasion and discipline techniques like the rehabilitation project force (imprisonment and forced labor), application of Hubbard's *Brainwashing Manual*, isolation or detachment from family, and similar procedures may be applied.[57] At this point, the Scientologist knows the rules of conduct and thought. Any independent thought, action, or questioning is considered "out-ethics" and can even lead to being declared a suppressive person

---

57 Atack, *A Piece of Blue Sky, Scientology, Dianetics and L. Ron Hubbard Exposed*, 452–456.

(the equivalent of being excommunicated). The Scientology euphemism for heretic is suppressive person or possibly "squirrel" (one who helps another in auditing without the permission of the church or alters the auditing process originally set forth by L. Ron Hubbard).

While the advanced org training continues to work its miracles on those who have enrolled in the OT levels of training, the higher levels of the church maintain and enforce doctrine, handle public relations, and monitor recruitment figures at the missions and the field offices. At this level, one would encounter the inner workings of the Church of Scientology through its various bureaucracies and front organizations. One might take note of the activities and secret bank accounts of the finance dictator and his finance police, entrusted to handle the income and investments of the church. The guardian office might employ its true believers as Sea Org operatives to implement Hubbard's fair game doctrine, identifying and seeking to destroy anyone or any group hostile to Scientology by any means available. The watch dog committee might be spying on potential suppressive persons or working on another high-level purge within the organization. If its past is any indication of its current mission and methods, the guardian office, acting as the intelligence arm of the church, would be conducting intelligence gathering activities, covert operations, and possible blackmailing of perceived enemies by infiltrating newspaper staffs, federal agencies, schools, law firms, and other key areas that allow the church access to otherwise confidential and personal information on those who would oppose it.

Sophisticated image control and propaganda, publishing, and other activities would all be directed from the organizational level of the church. Highly centralized in its control, the Church of Scientology passes on doctrine and directives to the missions for administrative purposes. The top levels of the church are not accountable to the franchised missions or rank and file of the church. Control of the church and accountability for its actions is hidden away at the top level of its management.

The sad history of the Church of Scientology and its abusive behavior and highly publicized lawsuits involving Paulette Cooper, the IRS, attorney Michael Flynn and his clients, Gerry Armstrong, and others is well documented. As the result of these legal battles, there are records available that document many of the ruthless tactics and actions taken by the church to suppress any derogatory information about its operations.

L. Ron Hubbard died (dropped his body) on January 24, 1986. He left the impression with his followers that in one of his many reincarnations, he was the Buddha. It's rather ironic in the sense that the Buddhist goal is that of disintegration of the self, whereas a Scientologist is consumed with the idea of total control over his or her self. He also claimed to be the reincarnation of Rawl, the imprisoner of the evil Xenu, and quite possibly, Cecil Rhodes. The future reincarnations of L. Ron Hubbard will allow him the time and space to continue his work for truth, justice, and the American way. Like the heroes in his novels, Ron will no doubt return in time to save the universe from oblivion. Hell has no claims on a man such as this.

Xenu is the guy I want to meet. Think of all those confused thetans floating around out there with no place to land except inside the minds of men. I put men's souls into God's Hell, but Xenu sent the reincarnated thetan souls to their own Hell: the mind of Man. What irony. What genius!

> *A good Scientologist does not question church authority, for to be a citizen of the "World of the Totally Free" is to obey.*
>
> —L. Ron Hubbard

Sympathy for the Devil

Most ignorance is vincible ignorance. We don't know because we don't want to know.

—Aldous Leonard Huxley

I am the lightning rod for religious beliefs. Most all religions invoke my name in one form or another to gain dependency of their faithful; but the warrior religions—and Christianity in particular—are the worst at using me as the primary scapegoat. Their believers have been programmed since birth to blame the devil for their transgressions and inability to resist temptations their religions tell them are sinful. The pot is certainly calling the kettle black.

Pick any time line in history and I can show you a period of political strife or war that is rooted in religion. A totally objective observer from some other planet might simply conclude that if so much evil on Earth stems from organized religion, perhaps religion is a creation of Satan to be used against mankind. Perhaps Satan has encouraged the concept of different and competing religions to create conditions on Earth that make his job much simpler than taking the elevator up from Hell a billion times daily to try to increase the population of Hell. Assuming Satan's goal is to acquire souls for Hell, this scenario would certainly make the job easier.

If each religion has the authority (as vested in them by God Almighty according to their respective church doctrines) to consign the believers of the competing religions to perdition, as well as having the ability to save their souls if converts would change their beliefs, all Satan has to do is find a place for all the souls that are damned by the religions of man to Hell. Mass damnation is much less work than tempting millions of individuals to do evil day in and day out. Simply sit back and let the church do Satan's work of filling God's Hell with the souls of men. It is a diabolical plan worthy of my reputation for cunning and treachery.

This little mind game has at least one flaw in its logic, however. I can't prove my innocence here, but my first rebuttal is that God is my master and, by nearly all accounts, my power is limited to tempting. I cannot compel anyone to do something against one's will.[58] If there is a Satan, there is a God; and God has set forth the rules of engagement. These rules do not allow me to usurp that which is holy in the eyes of God unless I have specific permission to do so (which I don't). If a religion is holy by God's definition, I have no power to direct or influence it. The question remains, of course, as to which religions are deemed holy in the eyes of God.

The assumption that my goal is to swell Hell's population is not valid. My job is to enlighten and illuminate people. Remember, according to Milton in *Paradise Lost*, I am Lucifer, the light bearer. There are so many myths and stories about why I exist that it is no wonder humanity is so confused about why things happen the way they do. Perhaps this is a good time to enlighten you as to my history. My inept public relations people have allowed others to define me for well over two thousand years, so I doubt that I can gain much sympathy for my cause. I don't think anyone has ever written anything positive about me, other than with tongue in cheek. Even the worshipers of Satan, whom I totally disavow, like to dwell on the imagined evil that

---

58 Russell, *Lucifer: The Devil in the Middle Ages*, 57.

they think I can bring down on their opponents. Nevertheless, I'll try to state my case as objectively and logically as possible.

Christians, not unlike the Jews, made it a practice to either absorb the gods of their allies and enemies into their ceremony and theology or turn the gods of their enemies into incarnations of the devil.[59] You won't find a biography or complete story about me in the Bible. Much of Christian mythology about me was inspired from Jewish pseudepigraphal sources including the Dead Sea Scrolls as well as from the Kabbalah. Noncanonical Christian apocryphal and gnostic texts also provide alternate versions of Hell and its heroes. Texts such as the Book of Enoch and the Testament of Solomon provided a basis from which others built until, by the seventeenth century, Christianity had pretty much completed its mosaic of the lords and princes that reigned in Hell.

Prevailing wisdom according to those who should know describes the hierarchy of Hell something like this:

Nine suborders of fallen angels, including cherubim and seraphim and other devils who make up the first hierarchy; a second hierarchy of dominions, principalities, and powers; and a third hierarchy that is populated by archangels and angels.

I, Satan (a.k.a. Lucifer), reign as lord of Hell, and my faithful Beelzebub is Prince of the First Hierarchy. If we were a democracy, I would be president and Beelzebub my vice president. The second hierarchy is ruled by Carreau, Prince of Powers, who uses the vice of pride to bring down souls. The third hierarchy is governed by Belias (Belial), Prince of Virtues. Belias has a fine knack for enlisting souls through their susceptibility to arrogance, contempt or ridicule. Other princes are in charge of the various deadly sins such as murder, sloth, envy, and so on.[60] The Jews have a slightly different version, but for the most part, the three hierarchies—each with three subhierarchies and a down line of orders and subdivisions populated with minor devils and demons—is the standard version of the empire of Hell.

59 Paine, *The Hierarchy of Hell*, 39–50, 53.
60 Ibid., 61–63.

The cast of players is legion! Remember Mammon? Moloch? Ashtoreth? Baal? There are scores of familiar names down here if you dig through the census. One man's god is another man's devil. If a god ever existed under another religion, you can bet I have him or her as a devil down here with me now. I would hope that somewhere a book exists with the genealogies of all my loyal subjects. Their origins truly make an interesting study for those obsessed with the power structure of Hell. Ancient gods of other religions have been transformed into evil spirits and cast into Hell. This religious transmutation of deities has provided me with most of my middle management.

Volumes have been written as to the makeup and nature of Hell and how man's perception of it has evolved over the centuries. I find it fascinating that intelligent and rational people will accept these mythical fantasies as gospel. If it exists at all, how would anyone ever really know what Hell is like? The myth of the archangel Michael and his fellow angels warring with me and the fallen angels who followed me down into Hell is from sources other than the Bible. It is not found in the New Testament (except for a brief reference to the fall of the angels in Revelations, obviously taken from a pseudepigraphal source); it is not found in the Old Testament. The Jewish Talmud never refers to me as leading evil spirits or fomenting a rebellion against God.

The Scroll of the War of the Sons of Light against the Sons of Darkness, found among the Dead Seas Scrolls near Qumran, provides an image of cosmic war between the forces of good against the forces of evil, but it does not name the leaders of the opposing forces. Neither the archangel Michael nor yours truly is named in this struggle.

Most of the basis of the myths about Hell comes from the author of the books of Enoch and the Gospel of Nicodemus. The First Book of Enoch and the Book of the Secrets of Enoch tell of the seven Heavens, the watchers, the fall of angels, and of the creation of evil. The Book of Jubilees tells another version of the angels' fall from Heaven. Revelations 12:7 tells us about a war that broke out in Heaven and how Michael and his angels fought against the "dragon," who is identified as "that ancient serpent, called the devil and Satan." But aside from referencing the war and fall of the angels, nothing about Hell is written in Revelations. The author of Revelations writes in allegory with heavy symbolic language about the "beast" and a host of nasty things to come, which shall ultimately end with Christ victorious, but there is considerable question as to whether he was referring to the Romans, Satan, Nero, or no one in particular as the object of his vilification.

If I am such a dreaded nemesis to Christians, why did the Christians wait so long to determine I was worthy of being included in their art and mythology? Christian art does not even portray me until AD 586.[61] I have always been hurt that they ignored me for so long. Was it because early Christianity had not yet fully developed their myth of Satan? Perhaps they did not realize that their religion could not survive without instilling fear, dread, and hate within the hearts of the faithful? That fear had to be directed at something or someone, and I was the chosen.

During the beginning of organized Christianity, the early Christians were busy just surviving and competing with other sects and established religions. Their leaders were being martyred, and they were busy killing each other while creating canon. The early Christians did not need to introduce any new antagonist threat to the church. Devils were still considered small stuff that any worthwhile prophet or exorcist could handle at the local level. There were higher priorities. Christians were enduring horrible persecutions during the early years of their history. These were the survival years for the Christian religion. Creating order within the church and competing for survival against pagan religions and Christian sects preaching heresies was more important at the time than saving souls from Satan.

Later, however, as Christianity became an ascendant religion (pun intended) over the pantheon of Greek and Roman deities that heretofore had dominated men's minds and having

---

61 Russell, *Satan: The Early Christian Tradition*, Preface page.

absorbed, suppressed, or crushed the Donatists, the Arians, the Ebionites, Mithraism, Nestorians, Jacobites, and a host of lesser known "heresies" or competing beliefs, they consolidated their gains and began to focus on what constituted canon within the church. As they added to the framework of Christian belief, they began to fill in some of the previously neglected areas of church philosophy.

The real prize for diabolical creativity goes to two Christian theologians: Irenaeus, Bishop of Lyons, and Tertullian, an influential Christian theologian who lived most of his life in Carthage. Both men lived during the late second century and wrote extensively about heresy, sin, and me. These men struggled with the fact that the Christian faith was riddled with heresies and feared that a church splintered with so many different interpretations of its theology would be doomed. So, to counter the evil of heresy, they promoted the idea that heresy is a sin brought about by the devil in his relentless war against Christ. I became the villain of an internecine war within the church. The doctrine they established against heresy and nonbelievers later brought us the Inquisition, holy wars, witch hunts, and the deadly persecution of anyone accused of nonconforming religious beliefs.[62] In other words, if you didn't believe what the church said you should believe, you were in league with Satan and his minions of Hell. And since you were among the damned, you could not be saved (contrary to the teachings of Jesus Christ) unless you recanted your heresy.

It seems obvious to me that the church was more in fear of losing its ecumenical grip on Christ's true believers than losing those souls to Hell. I probably gained more souls from damnation by the church than I ever gained recruiting on my own!

The concept of the devil goes back to the beginnings of mankind. Man has always feared the unknown and felt vulnerable to the natural forces of the universe. When good things happened to the tribes or cities, the gods were pleased and had blessed them with the fruits of their grace. When bad

---

62 Pagels, *The Origins of Satan*, 163–166.

things happened, something had displeased the gods. When drought threatened to turn their crops to dust, the gods must be angry. When storms and floods raged, men offered appeasing sacrifices to the storm gods. Drought, floods, famine, pestilence, death, war, or any other man-made or natural disaster meant the gods were angry and must be placated. Whenever anything that threatened men's existence occurred, the ancients turned to their gods.

The warrior religions, however, consider themselves monotheistic. That is to say, there is but one God, and He is omnipotent and good. So when bad things happen to a monotheist, it must be the work of the devil and his minions. Of course, over the centuries, the pagan gods have evolved into the pantheon of minor devils that make up Hell's hierarchy of fallen angels. Some of the names have been altered slightly due to linguistic translations and other permutations, but the villains are still the same old gods of the past. Thus, in an ironic twist, *those same gods that the ancients feared became the devils that the monotheists fear.*

In summary, details about the origins of Hell and Satan come not from the Bible but from sources outside the Bible. Much of this literature is allegorical or metaphorical yet taken quite literally by those who have accepted the mythology of Hell as an integral part of their religious belief. My point here is not that evil does not exist, but that Hell and the Devil are mythical creations that have evolved over the centuries as a backdrop to religions that depend on fear of damnation and the eternal fires of Hell to maintain their hold on the faithful. These religions are based on fear rather than altruistic works of good or spiritual self-improvement. To an independent thinker, they are ignoble.

The demagogue is one who preaches doctrines he knows to be untrue to men he knows to be idiots.
—H. L. Mencken

The Defense Rests

*When the fight begins within himself, a man's
worth something.*
—Robert Browning

I have covered, in very general terms, the theologies and
doctrines of the major religions and beliefs of man. There have
been countless volumes of text written against and in defense
of each of these religions. After reading several volumes on each
topic, one will discover that they all tend to have one thing in
common, and that is the reaction of the true believer. *In the event
of overwhelming evidence or lack of a rational reply, the defenders
of the faith can always withdraw to the comfort and safety of their
"faith."* For the true believer, faith is the castle's keep. In the
universe of the true believer, anything that threatens or attacks
in any way his or her religious belief represents the forces of
darkness. The true believer will continue to wage his war against
Satan and the perceived forces of evil because that is what he
was taught and that is what he believes.

The historian, the scientist, the anthropologist, and others
who would produce information that threatens or does not
support the theology as taught by a particular religion may
be attacked or ignored. If the discovery doesn't threaten the
theology, they will generally be ignored by religious authorities.

Their views or discoveries will be accepted and even promoted when and if they support certain theological claims. But should their discovery, theory, or interpretation of evidence threaten an accepted religious belief, the scholar or scientist will have his reputation attacked and his theories subjected to ridicule. It is the nature of the scientific community to vigorously attack or at least shun and disassociate themselves from radical or interpretive discoveries that do not reinforce the scientific community's preconceived ideas. Religions react the same way. This practice of attacking the source is effective to the degree of power the religion can exercise over its community versus the reputation of the person being attacked. Galileo was not the first nor was he the last to recant a scientific truth to satisfy religious dogma.

Over time, educational history books change their focus and eliminate events that negatively impact religious thought and belief. This is sometimes done on purpose, but usually it simply happens because cultural and political forces make it more convenient to omit the telling of such events than to highlight the dark side of a mainstream religion. Catholic atrocities in the seventeenth and eighteenth centuries to Native Amerindians, Polynesians, and indigenous populations in the Caribbean have been whitewashed or eliminated from school textbooks. The intolerance of the early Puritans and the savagery they demonstrated against Quakers and other religious groups coming to the British Crown Colonies in the Americas is no longer printed in high school textbooks. Muslim-instilled violence in Africa and in the Near and Far East against other religions gets little attention in Western textbooks. The world is a nasty place. Unfortunately, the bland tripe that passes for history in modern society will never reveal the evils that lurk in the dark recesses of world events.

The true believers are not going to change their minds just because some facts profess to expose fault with a doctrine they have given their hearts and minds to. The true believer's mind is closed to all but the familiar doctrine he or she has been exposed to since birth or conversion. Too much effort has gone into believing one's theology to accept the fact that it might not be true or is not the Word of God. How can one who has accepted a doctrine as the gospel suddenly accept that there are major flaws in the theology? The fact is, they can't and they don't.

To the true believer, I can only ask that you don't blame me for all the ills of the world. God created the universe and all that is in it. God created me for a purpose known only to Him. I am the subservient and willing tool of an omnipotent God, and I exist only at His pleasure. Don't close your mind to the universe that God created for you. Explore it.

To the true believer, then, I ask that you take responsibility for your life and don't blame your inadequacies on me. If I exist, then I exist because God created me. The Creator can also destroy me. If that was His will, it would have been done by now. So live and believe as you would, but don't cry out, "This is the work of Satan!" every time you or your belief is threatened. Perhaps it's just the Will of God.

> *What men usually ask of God when they pray is that two and two not make four.*
> —Anonymous

Epilogue

In religion and politics, people's beliefs and convictions are in almost every case gotten at second-hand, and without examination.
—Mark Twain

What you have read here is a primer to the information that awaits you if you simply take the time to look for it. "The truth is out there somewhere" it is said. Someone else said "the truth shall set you free." Whatever the "truth" is, and if it really exists at all, you should know by now it will not simply come to you. You must seek it out and apply enormous critical thought to the information and your conclusions. If you are serious in your search for the "truth," you will not accept dogmatic answers or incomplete theologies. You will be persistent in your questions and not accept scholastic sounding, incomprehensible mumbo jumbo or faulty reasoning.

There are truly devils and demons out there. But the demons originate from the minds of men and are subject to the will of each individual who might encounter such a fiend. There are demons of the mind, there are demons of destruction, and there are demons who are disguised as friendly angels. They may be called jinn, they may be called thetans, or they may be called devils. God allows such demons to exist because that's the way

He designed man's mind and his world. But God didn't have to create the demons; man took care of that task without God's help.

Hopefully, out of all the topics we have covered thus far, I've left you with at least one thing to ponder. If so, my endeavors here have been successful. The meme is planted and I now take my leave on the subjects of organized religion, holy books, myths and Hell.

But my work here is not yet finished. Since I still have your attention, may I suggest you continue our little journey by reading the essays my minions and I have put together in Book II of this tome? We invite you to join us in exploring some of the belief principles and logical frailties of mankind that lead to the human condition.

If not, until we meet again, please accept the very warmest regards from yours truly, the Prince of Darkness and Lord of Hell.

> *A dogma will thrive in soil where the truth could not get root.*
> —Lemuel K. Washburn

BOOK II
SATAN'S SOLILOQUY

Essays of a Diabolical Nature

Faced with religious uncertainty and various deities from which to choose, man will profess belief in the deity that most terrifies him, knowing that if his choice is wrong the consequences are minimal. If by some chance, however, the god of his chosen religion does actually exist, his chances of personal survival and reward are greatly enhanced.

—Satan

The Origin of Evil

The only demons that exist in this world are in the minds of men.

—Zog

Some say the origin of all evil is the devil. I, Satan, submit that evil's origin was created when God created the living, conscious creatures of the earth. Furthermore, *evil cannot exist unless a conscious being exists to create and act upon it.* Without a conscious mind to incubate evil, it does not exist. It is not a virus that lies inert upon the earth or that dwells in Hell, waiting to infect its victim. It is not conjured up by demons or the devil and thrust upon some poor, unsuspecting creature. Evil exists only by virtue of the existence of a conscious mind created by God that may or may not be rational, with an intellect that can conceive of the deed but may or may not be aware that it is defined as evil.

Evil is not confined to dark, satanic forces that fight against good. It is not a force that exists outside the consciousness of man. Evil is everywhere men reside. Zealots and extremists often take a benevolent concept and turn it into a vehicle of horror. A quick primer in church history will show that what we know as evil has origins from both the saints as well as the sinners. The terrible deeds and human suffering promoted by that Christian institution known as the Inquisition were the direct results of the Roman Catholic Church. I was not involved with Mohammed's massacres and killings. Such wars are not fought in the name of Satan; they are deemed "holy" by those religious fanatics who take up the sword for their God. It was not Satan, but rather it was the *fear of* Satan and carelessly interpreted verses in the Bible that prompted Christians to mercilessly kill and torture women accused as witches.

As related in the Book of Genesis (3:4–5) in the Bible, when Adam ate of the Tree of Knowledge, he was then able to know the difference between good and evil. Thus it stands that evil (as it is understood biblically) had already been created by God and existed at the time of Adam's "sin" of disobeying God's directive.

I did not create evil. Evil, as is its concept and its definition, is in the mind of man. There can be no evil unless a conscious mind is present to create it and to recognize it. The mind of man is an integral part of God's creation. Thus the origin of evil is God. This doesn't mean that God is evil; it merely reminds the true believer that an omnipotent god created the universes and the heavens and all that is contained within them. No exceptions. If evil exists, God created it. If, however, as some will argue, God is a creation of man, then evil is likewise a creation of man. And of course, ipso facto, so am I. I submit, therefore, that whatever wickedness and evil this way comes, it comes not from me.

> *The belief in a supernatural source of evil is not necessary; men alone are quite capable of every wickedness.*
> —Joseph Conrad

Evil as Defined by the Mind of Man

Reality is the other person's idea of how things should be.

—John M. Shanahan

Before we can further explore the concept of evil, we must first define what it is we wish to examine. The term "right" (as opposed to wrong) does not necessarily mean it is not evil or bad. "Right" and "wrong" are terms that denote degrees of cultural correctness as measured by different standards over time and geography. What was once determined as "right" in the eyes of the ancients may not be considered appropriate (or "right") by today's standards. The terms "good" and "bad" are similarly measured by local custom as well as by moral standards and beliefs of the day. A bad deed is not necessarily an evil deed. An act of sin is not necessarily an act of evil. All such absolutes defining morality such as good, bad, right, wrong, evil, etc. are actually subjective terms that depend upon how they are defined. Philosophical absolutes are an illusion.

The concept of evil denotes something of a morally negative characteristic. It is not good, and it cannot by definition be holy. But the term must still be defined by the user, who may have diametrically opposed ideas to his adversary as to what is "good" and what is "evil."

If you believe that your god requires and even demands a human sacrifice, are you wrong to kill a victim to satisfy your god? An Aztec priest would tell you that you have done the right thing; it is good to appease your god and obey your faith even if you are personally repulsed at the deed. Others would tell you that to murder someone for any purpose is morally wrong and is a bad thing to do. The God of the Old Testament killed legions of people in various rages and fits of anger. (Check out 1 Chronicles 21:2, 7, 14 for just one example.) Was this an evil act on the part of God? (First Chronicles 21:15 implies it was.)

It may be considered "right" by a priest, rabbi, cleric, or imam and may even be sanctioned by one's religious doctrine to kill unarmed civilians who are nonbelievers. Others would argue that it is wrong to kill for that reason. Those who condemn such action might, however, approve of killing a criminal who has broken certain secular laws. So which law is "right" and which is "wrong"? Which is bad and which is good? Is it evil to do the bidding of one's chosen god, even if it means taking the lives of innocent beings or beings who do not share your belief? How absolute, then, is the concept of evil?

If evil were absolute—if it could be universally defined and categorized without exception—it would not be the subject of so many literary works. But the concept of evil is not so easy to grasp. Instinctively, one would state that if a deed is so horrible, so criminally violent it defies description, it must by definition be evil. When someone or some group performs some hideous deed, it is easy to make the statement that "this was an evil deed that must be punished." Yet, to the perpetrators (who do not see themselves as evil), this deed was an act of revenge, war, or in some other way justified, even sanctified, in their minds.

Since the beginning of time, terrible things have been done by men to their fellow beings. The Assyrian Sennacherib slaughtered all the inhabitants of Babylon when his army took the city in 689 BCE. Similar evils have been repeated countless times over history by various emperors and kings. The Old Testament is replete with examples of Israelite atrocities committed against their "enemies." The Roman Church's Inquisition conducted horrid acts against those condemned for heresy. The 1937 Japanese rape of Nanking saw the slaughter of tens of thousands of Chinese civilians, torturing of innocent women and children, forced gang rape of an estimated twenty thousand women held in pens for sexual abuse by Japanese soldiers, and similar outrages against humanity. Nazis in Germany enslaved and murdered millions of Jews during World War II. Religious terrorists continue to conduct suicidal acts of destruction and mayhem against innocent people. Are the horrible deeds of these groups and individuals evil? Were they inspired by satanic forces?

The Assyrians were building an empire and were ruthless toward opposition. Babylon opposed them, and the Assyrians destroyed the city. The destruction of Babylon was considered an example to all others who might oppose them, and the devastation was designed to eliminate a potential adversary. To the Assyrians, the killing of the inhabitants of Babylon was not evil, but a necessary act of survival and conquest. The Jews of the Old Testament were frequently told by their god, YHWH, to kill the thousands of men, women, and children of the tribes and kingdoms they defeated in battle. Their acts of genocide were based upon the instructions of God and immediately eliminated the potential of intertribal hatred that might seed future acts of revenge by the conquered. The Roman Church was trying to root out the evils of heresy, sorcery, and witchcraft for the good of humanity and to save souls from Hell. The Japanese troops were exacting revenge upon the Chinese and venting their losses and frustrations during an intense period of wartime. The Nazis were eliminating Jews whom, for a number of reasons, they accused of being an internal danger to the fatherland and the Aryan race. They were keeping the non-Jewish Caucasian race pure and ridding the world of something they considered was a blight on humanity. Religious terrorists are convinced they are fighting against an evil force and that their cause is just and right. The acts of all these participants may seem evil to the majority of humans, but in the eyes of the perpetrators the results are wrapped in justifiable causes.

Can a cause or crusade that is held as just and true in the eyes of the beholder be evil? Has Satan veiled the minds of these crusaders? Can Satan be blamed for the terrible deeds that are committed in the name of causes that are perceived by some as just and good? And, regardless of our revulsion, if that cause is just in the mind of a single individual rather than adopted by an entire group of the same persuasion, is it then to be considered evil simply because only one man believes in the righteousness of his personal cause? In other words, given an analogous belief, is the individual evil but the group sanctified?

Evil may be associated with Satan but it should not be synonymous with Satan. As stated earlier, assuming I truly do exist, I am the creation of God. More to the fact, like the concept of evil, I am actually a creation of the mind of man. The concept of evil is intuitive but cannot be easily explained when rationally approached. Evil does not exist as a force or power unto itself. Evil exists as a concept, but it does not exist in any identifiable form. The idea of evil is universally perceived by mankind, but evil itself cannot be tangibly identified by mankind because it is conceived by men and will be defined by those same men. And they will likely define evil as something vile, corrupt, and definitely as something contrary to their beliefs and values. Evil lurks in the minds of men, and there it must be examined.

The mind of man is intellectual enough to both understand the concept of evil and to rationalize its own actions so that it is never guilty of evil. Everything is relative in the minds of men. The evils cited earlier in this essay, at least to the perpetrators, were justified. What is more unsettling is that hidden beneath the "justifiable" excuses or exculpation are the real reasons for these "evils."

The real motives for such horrible atrocities lie buried in the consciousness of the men who willingly perform such acts of depravity. The ancient kings wanted power and used whatever tactics necessary to obtain and hold it. The priesthood wanted to perpetuate itself, so in many cases the prophets and priests provided the moral cover necessary for the king to inflict terrible atrocities upon his fellow human beings. Soldiers in war know the boundaries of civilized behavior but under the stresses and horror of war they may often succumb to their baser natures to mask their pain and experience pleasure in whatever deviant form it may come. The terrorist may be torn by a multitude of internal conflicts or simply wish to gain fame and notoriety; in any case, he will give up his life and the lives of those around him to satisfy his ego or his guilt. These and similar hidden motives run parallel to the announced motives given by depraved human beings who act with malevolence and barbarism.

By design or evolution, mankind has been blessed or cursed with three brains: the reptilian brain; the mammalian brain; and the human neocortex, or cerebellum, which is split into two hemispheres like the right and left halves of a walnut. They are all housed inside the skull, one layer on top of the other.[63]

The brain is a complex organ that makes man what he is. Sane and rational or insane and irrational, eccentric or "normal," whatever genetics, experiences, and environment that shape a man's thoughts make him what he is. The brain enables man to rationalize his actions or act out aggression, unconscious of what is really motivating him. A man could be considered an evil menace to society yet in his own mind he thinks he is fulfilling God's work. Buried in his subconscious, however, he may actually be rebelling against a society that he has personalized so that he may wreck his revenge upon it.

The mind of man is a complex enigma, and it defies man's complete understanding. It is dependent upon organic tissue that chemically generates electrical impulses that allow the body to function independent of conscious thought. This tissue, called the brain, directs the body's movements, determines which survival traits the body will adopt in any given situation, generates thoughts, stores information and memories, solves

---

63 Sagan, *The Dragons of Eden*, 55–57.

problems, creates ideas, hallucinates, and performs a host of other critical and not so critical tasks.

The mind created by the human brain is holistic, multidimensional, not always rational, and is imbued with both real and false memories. The many tenebrous traits of the mind often dictate the direction of the consciousness it controls. Frequently, the mind is influenced more by its environment and the ideas it has been exposed to than from its own independent logic. The human mind is a faulty piece of work and can be depended upon to produce faulty conclusions because of how it interprets and processes information.

Man rationalizes his thoughts and acts by dredging up information stored in his brain and processing that data to fit his wants and needs. His interpretation of the data is generally biased in favor of his expectations or desires. Man's attempts at logic are often fraught with false assumptions, biased choices of information, or leaps of faith. Scientists are guilty of this. Theologians are guilty of this. Humanity is guilty of this.

True believers who insist that Satan is behind the evils of the world base their conclusion on the assumption that Satan exists and is evil incarnate. They accuse others of doing the works of Satan when those deeds and beliefs do not conform with their own. They blame demons that possess living creatures for the evils that men do. Their theology needs to validate the concept of evil as a supernatural force that can only be overcome by their god. Satan is their way to personify the concept of evil. A hierarchy of Hell filled with myths, devils, jinn, and demons is created as a foundation from which the theologist can satisfactorily explain the origin of evil without implicating God. It is the theodicy of the warrior religions.

There truly are demons of the mind, of course. But these demons are not supernatural; they exist as conflicts between the holistic elements of the brain, which are working at cross-purposes with each other. The origin of such "demons" is physiological conditions that produce hallucinations, irrational thought, delusions, insanity, and all sorts of psychosis. They are spiritual only in context to the explanation given by the examiner as to who is to blame for the mental contention going on within the mind of the conflicted. The conflicted is possessed by his own mind, not by demons of Hell.

The mind is its own place, and in itself can make a heaven of Hell, a hell of Heaven.

—John Milton

The Concept of Good and Evil

There are no philosophical absolutes. Such concepts as truth, reality, good, and evil are illusions that do not exist outside of man's imagination.

—Zog

I partially disagree with Zog. The concept of evil is absolute *based on our perception of reality*. Although we cannot absolutely know evil, we can at least perceive evil as an absolute. There are some concepts and laws that exist outside man's ability to recognize them. We sense them, but we cannot isolate, define, and truly know them. Without man's ability to imagine and think, I agree that evil would not exist for him. Evil would be present in the world so long as there were sentient beings that could conceive and implement acts of harm to other conscious beings. Nevertheless, with or without the consciousness of man, the concept of evil would still exist in the universe, waiting for discovery.

Evil is not unlike a natural law that exists but remains incomprehensible to the intellect of man. It has yet to be properly identified and defined by man. Man sees the results of evil all around him but cannot identify its source or properly define it due to the inherent subjectivity that surrounds its definition. Defining evil is similar to trying to grasp the concept of eternity. The abstractions are known, but they cannot be fully comprehended by the mind of man. Just as eternity can be considered an absolute, so can the concept of evil. Zog is in error when he makes the claim that there are no philosophical absolutes outside of man's imagination. To the contrary, the absolutes exist; man, however, simply cannot comprehend them.

Evil is thought to be universally recognized by all sane humans. But oddly enough, evil is not always recognized for what it is and is not always illegal or immoral by society's dictates. Something that is evil should be a sin, regardless of religious doctrine, and it should violate all secular law. But it is not, and it does not. We cannot know evil, we can only perceive it.

If God did not exist, evil would still be present among us. The concept of evil does not depend upon the existence of God. Theodicy becomes an issue only because true believers and some philosophers feel the need to defend the fact that evil seems to exist in tandem with their god.

A sin is something that goes against your faith's doctrine. That doctrine may include condemning acts that are universally deemed as deviant behavior. But not all sin is necessarily evil. It may be considered a sin not to believe a particular religion's doctrine (heresy), but only a fanatic would argue that such a sin is evil. Sloth is considered a sin by some; it's a bad habit, but is it really an evil trait? Sins are transgressions that can be measured incrementally, and most are simply failures of the human condition as measured against a religious doctrine. Most are benign actions that take place in everyday activities of human intercourse. "The devil made me do it," is the tongue in cheek response to such lapses of conduct. Of course, there are the terrible sins against humanity committed by the morally deviant as well as doctrinal sins that one's religion considers unpardonable against God and the faith.

A rock is an inanimate object. It is neither good nor evil. It has no morality traits at all. Depending on its location, size, and shape, it could be very beneficial to a person. It could help complete a wall of a home under construction; it could help dam up a creek and allow for irrigation of a farmer's crop and livestock; or it could be used to grind grain and make food. Is the rock "good"?

That same rock might also be used as a boulder to be rolled down upon an enemy or victim moving through a pass below; it could be used as the tip of a spear to kill or rob someone; or its mineral content could be used to create a terrible weapon or poison. Is the rock "bad"? Is it evil?

The rock is neither good nor bad. Until a use was conceived for the rock by a sentient being, it was morally sterile. Once a conscious entity put the rock to a use, it became an instrument of the intelligence that put it to use. If that use was for an evil purpose, the being using the rock is evil, not the rock itself.

The rock, perched high up on a mountain, could suffer erosion at its base until it finally surrenders to the pull of gravity and rolls down the mountain. The rock could start a landslide that creates a natural lake, which benefits all creatures in the area. Or it could carry tons of stone and earth down upon a sleeping village with terrible consequences to the inhabitants below. In both scenarios, because nature interfered with the inanimate nature of the rock, the effects of the rock's movement had a radical effect. Is the rock good or bad? Was the result due to nature or God? Are nature and God one and the same? If the results were beneficial, was it God's blessing? If the results were catastrophic, was it God's curse on those below or the work of the devil?

There is no such thing as "natural evil." The forces of nature are neutral in the affairs of man. The physical properties of the universe were established when creation occurred, and they are not subject to change by evil forces. Assuming God created the earth and all that is upon it, it stands to reason that nature is an inherent part of the earth. If God's work in seven days creating the universe and the world was good in the eyes of God, I submit that God created that which we call nature. If God created nature as part of His creation, I cannot take credit or blame for acts of nature. Natural disasters are called "acts of God" by many, not "acts of the devil."

The simple fact of the matter is that evil is not found in inanimate objects nor is it created by storm gods rampaging across the planet wreaking havoc on the possessions of men. Natural disasters are called *natural* because they are the result of phenomena occurring naturally upon the earth. They are part of God's design for the planets and the universe. These are God's own immutable laws of the universe.

Laws, religion, and personal morality help us define and identify the concept we know as evil, but they are all subjective. There are different interpretations of what is right and what is legal. There are unjust laws and laws that seem immoral to some. The law is a tool man uses for his own means. Legality is a subjective term that has nothing to do with the definition of evil.

Sin is not absolute because it depends on which doctrine of faith one lives by. The Islamic doctrine tells its true believer that it is his duty to slay the infidel. This is an act of murder against a non-Muslim person. To the Muslim, it is not a sin; to the Christian, it is a sin. The concept of sin is subjective and based on ecclesiastical law. What is pure, righteous, and holy in the eyes of God? What is evil in the eyes of God? Who speaks for God?

Individual morality can recognize evil, but it, too, is subjective. The level of the moral plane helps define the degree of spirituality of an individual. That individual may define evil within the context of his or her own level of spirituality. But any such personal morality, however moral and virtuous, is still not an absolute measurement because of the imperfection of the individual. The concept of evil is still subject to the level of spirituality achieved by the moral person. The moral person's interpretation of evil is filtered through his or her life experiences. Personal experience leads to biases. Two people can contemplate the same act and one's conscience may tell him that what he is about to do is not only wrong, but evil. The other individual, devoid of the level of morality exhibited by the former and free of any religious issues that might otherwise restrain him, has no pangs of conscience and sees no evil in what he is about to do.

Evil should be an absolute concept that is not subject to interpretive differences as measured by man. Evil is the concept of the lack of morality with conscious intent to do harm to other sentient beings. Is the purported evil illegal, immoral, obscene, an atrocity, a sin against one's god—or something else? Using such terms to describe evil gives the concept a subjective nature. How do we recognize it and its source?

Evil does not occur without the help of a sentient being. Evil can only exist where there is consciousness. Evil is spawned from the consciousness of living creatures, and mankind is the primary sentient being on Earth. Other animals have brains, can think, and are susceptible to evil deeds, also, but their evils are limited in scope. Man, however, has the intellect and the ability to use tools to create greater evil. Mankind must bear the responsibility for nearly all evil in the world.

Evil lurks within the minds of men, and it is not put there by me. God gave men free will; by that act of God, man must bear the responsibility of his thoughts and actions. I cannot prove to the true believer that I do not whisper temptations into the hearts and minds of men that lead them to unspeakable evils. But remember that God created me as His adversary for man. He limited my abilities to do any harm to man without His authorization. Read closely the Book of Job in the Bible. It was God that brought up the topic of Job with me. After God took from Job all of his worldly possessions and family, He then told me to do my best to make poor Job lose faith. I did as I was directed, and God handled the rest.

As was my cosmic role (according to Christian doctrine) in the time line of man's history, I tempted Christ a time or two, but I didn't tell Him to lose His temper and throw all the moneychangers out of the temple. Unlike the role given to poor Judas, I didn't have anything to do with His crucifixion.

The Genesis myth tells of the story of Adam and Eve, whereby they eat of the fruit of the tree of knowledge of good and evil after being tempted by the serpent—not Satan or the devil, but "the *serpent* [who] was more crafty than any other wild animal that the Lord God had made" (Gen. 3:1(NRSV). I wasn't even present at the Garden of Eden. This is the ancient Jewish allegory of man's awareness of himself and the world around him (i.e., obtaining consciousness and the ability to know right from wrong). From this point on, evil existed in the world because it was in the mind of man. God created man, man creates evil. The origin of evil must go to the source of creation.

Any conscious being is susceptible to thoughts of evil without my assistance. I can only tempt a man to follow up on his base desires or depraved plans. Man generates a thought, I can only tempt, and then man acts on his thoughts according to his own free will. The human imagination is unlimited in its ability to conceive abominations upon his fellow human being. Humanity doesn't need me to justify the extent of the horrors it inflicts upon itself. That's what free will is all about, isn't it?

> *EVIL: That which one believes of others. It is a sin to believe evil of others, but it is seldom a mistake.*
> —H. L. Mencken

The Nature of Man's Laws

Satan: one of the Creator's lamentable mistakes, repented in sashcloth and axes. Being instated as an archangel, Satan made himself multifariously objectionable and was finally expelled from Heaven. Halfway in his descent he paused, bent his head in thought a moment, and at last went back. "There is one favor that I should like to ask," said he.

"Name it."

"Man, I understand, is about to be created. He will need laws."

"What, wretch! You, his appointed adversary, charged from the dawn of eternity with hatred of his soul—you ask for the right to make his laws?"

"Pardon; what I have to ask is that he be permitted to make them himself."

It was so ordered.
        —Ambrose Bierce, *The Devil's Dictionary*

I maintain that there are four primary types of laws created or recognized by mankind: First is moral law, encompassing mankind's basic rules of proper conduct that should be self-evident by their lack of injury to any sentient being. Second are the administrative laws, which sets forth the rules of commerce and general conduct of citizens among themselves. Third are political laws that have nothing to do with morality or administrative rules but are established to allow some men to have power or leverage over others or protect a hegemony. Fourth are ecclesiastical laws, which are set down by religious organizations to be followed by those who are practicing members of such faiths.

Moral law supersedes administrative, political and ecclesiastical laws; it is fixed and not subject to change. Administrative laws should but do not always supersede political laws; they are the laws that allow a community to maintain order and provide a framework within which to conduct its business. Political laws are those laws that are created and repealed over time as the power spectrum shifts; they are rules for the governed but not necessary to maintain order in a society. One may break an administrative or political law and not sin, but breaking a moral law will generally be a sin or create negative karma under most religious doctrines. A political law is a law that may be legally binding but could be morally reprehensible. Ecclesiastical law is often confused with moral law. Ecclesiastical law is confined by the doctrine of one's faith and does not always meet the higher standards of moral law. Even though ecclesiastical law professes to be based on morality, it is frequently self-serving, suffers from bias, and is subject to change as culture and beliefs evolve.

Moral Law

Man has invented his own reality through religion. Heaven and Hell are man-made devices designed to create an illusory reality apart from God's reality. We must not try to mold our ideas of reality and perfection to suit our religious or philosophical tastes.

—Satan

Moral law represents a universal, abstract concept incomprehensible to man and is not to be confused with morality, which reflects the more subjective concept of righteousness, and is a doctrine of moral conduct as set forth by differing cultures. Like the earlier analogy of evil and eternity as absolutes that cannot be intellectually comprehended, moral law exists at a level beyond what men define as moral laws. Men make moral laws; moral law, like the law of gravity, exists with or without the blessings of man.

Moral law transcends laws set forth by men. Unlike the other laws of men, moral law is not a creation of mankind; its existence is simply recognized by those who have reached a high enough level of awareness to comprehend the concept. It is an abstract concept that is absolute to the extent it can only be recognized by what might be referred to as spiritual man.

Unfortunately, spiritual man is also an abstract concept and does not exist except in the imagination of man. Thus morality is not an absolute term in the context of what we perceive as reality, but moral law as an abstract concept is absolute on a cosmic scale.

Man's mind is by nature subjective, and the subjectivity of man's mind does not allow it to comprehend a philosophical absolute. Man can imagine the concept of a philosophical absolute and he may even grasp pieces of the concept, but he can neither accurately define it in its totality nor can he recognize it in its entirety. A philosophical absolute must, because of man's subjective nature, exist outside the realm of man's epistemological abilities. There are truths beyond our understanding, and it is only there that absolutes can be found. For example, the concept of infinity might be understood by a person through the use of mathematical symbols used to represent the concept, but no one has the intellect to be able to fully appreciate its significance or visualize infinity in his mind.

Moral law, taken in context with our limited ability to recognize it, is praised by many, sought by most, practiced by few, and recognized by even fewer. The concept of moral law is beyond man's ability to recognize and define it as an absolute, based on our limited perception of reality. Unlike the three types of law created by man, moral law is immutable and universal on a cosmic level. It is not a creation of man; it is not unlike a natural law of the universe, waiting to be discovered by those spiritually advanced enough to recognize it for what it is. Moral law, unlike ecclesiastical law, does not require a belief in God. It is the highest plane of the four laws devised or recognized by man.

Moral law, unlike the concept of morality, is not dependent upon the subjectivity of the person or persons passing moral judgment. Moral laws are very basic acts of conduct within the scope of human conscience. The simplest way to determine if an act is a moral act is to ask the question, "Did this act cause harm to a living being?" Even a person without conscience cannot credibly argue that his act of theft, murder, deceit, or whatever did not harm the victim. He can argue that the victim was deserving of the act and that his conscience is clear or even that "the devil made him do it" or "God told him to do it," but in any case his act caused harm to his victim and was a breach of moral law. If his act remains undiscovered, he has still broken moral law. If discovered by the community in which he committed his act, administrative law may be applied to punish him.

The highest level of morality man can imagine is derived from a moral code of conduct of his own devising, most of which is based upon the mores and values as set forth by the institutions he created. Moral law represents an abstract level of conduct that is beyond man's ability to fully recognize and understand. Moral law is absolute and immutable; morality is subjective.

If I rape, pillage, and plunder *my own people*, I have violated a moral law, an administrative law, and probably an ecclesiastical law. If I rape, pillage, and plunder nonbelievers under the auspices of my faith, I am guilty of breaking a moral law but not the ecclesiastical law of my faith, which espouses such action. Moral law transcends ecclesiastical law, since ecclesiastical law is subject to interpretation of religious doctrine and debate. Moral law requires an inherent sense of right and wrong and is constant, regardless of denominational faith, culture, or circumstances. Moral law represents the highest authority of conduct and the ultimate good.

Moral law is secular and covers basic tenets of moral conduct. For example, stealing from a member of one's community is morally wrong. There are no exceptions. Someone is hurt by this action. Such an act betrays a common trust and invites retribution by the community to eliminate any future acts of theft. The community cannot survive if theft is allowed to exist unpunished. The community might even pass an administrative law to define the punishment for violating this moral law. But even without an administrative or ecclesiastical law against theft, the act of theft is still morally wrong. We don't steal, we don't kill our friends and neighbors; we don't do things that are considered morally deviant within our own society and that are repugnant to our individual consciences. We don't do things that unnecessarily harm other living beings. To do otherwise is to violate moral law.

> *Be careful how you interpret the world; it is like that.*
>
> —Erich Heller

Administrative Law

And God said: "Let there be Satan, so people don't blame everything on me. And let there be lawyers, so people don't blame everything on Satan."
—John Wing

Administrative laws are those rules set forth by the ruling civil authorities so that order can be maintained and those governed can conduct their business within the framework of the law of the land. Each community may have different laws and punishments covering the same offenses. If I wish to build a home, I may have to obtain permits from the governing body so that my home does not violate certain covenants or zoning rules. This protects my neighbors from any haphazard project that might cause them inconvenience or threaten their property values. If I get a ticket for speeding, I have violated an administrative law. Speed limits and traffic laws are imposed to promote safety for those who are using the highway.

Administrative laws sometimes incorporate ecclesiastical laws into their legal code. For example, requiring a business to close on a Sunday is an administrative law that is based on ecclesiastical law forbidding work on the Sabbath. The forbidding of liquor sales on Sunday while allowing other retail establishments and restaurants to conduct their business as normal is the imposition of ecclesiastical morality on the governed even though there is no ecclesiastical law that allows one while forbidding the other.

Administrative laws can often conflict with all three of the other types of law. For example, the law of the land may allow me to own slaves. I may even mistreat them unless administrative law dictates guidelines to that effect. If members of my community believe it is their moral duty to steal my slaves from me for the purpose of setting them free, they are violating administrative law and can be punished. Ecclesiastical law is ambivalent toward the institution of slavery, so to some I am breaking both moral and ecclesiastical law, and to others it's acceptable conduct. Politically, some in my community strongly disagree with my ownership of slaves because it reduces available paying jobs that might otherwise go to working members of the community. These people seek to pass political laws that, while popular to many, are designed to restrict my property rights for reasons other than moral issues. Morally, I may believe I am providing food and shelter to my slaves, protecting them from their inability to survive in the community. Others, however, maintain that I am breaking a moral law by depriving these slaves of the right to be free to live their lives as they see fit.

The conundrum here is which law prevails. My rights are protected by administrative law; ecclesiastical law is unclear, political law in this example is misguided, and moral law depends on the point of view of the two sides of the slavery issue. While it may be easy to take the politically correct high road and say the antislavery position is the morally correct position, one must not jump to conclusions. What moral law has been broken?

Both sides have a case. The slave owner may realize that his slaves are uneducated, illiterate, and cannot speak the language of the community. They simply do not have the skills to survive on their own in the community and, though they'd be free in the sense that they were no longer slaves, they would likely be economically and even physically abused by less savory members of the community. On the other hand, the antislavery members of the community maintain and feel strongly that to keep a person in bondage against his or her will is obviously immoral. Both positions feel they are on morally solid ground. The antislavery people would take the slave owner's property and set the slaves free to live their lives as free members of the community. The slave owner would not only be deprived of his property, but would fear for the welfare of those slaves set free, exchanging one type of bondage for another.

Of course the moral dilemma isn't quite as black and white as it may appear. A moral law was broken by whoever originally enslaved these people. It could have been parents who sold their own children into slavery or slave traders who abducted them who violated a moral law and set events into place. The original enslavement could have been from a tribal conflict, whereby the conquerors enslaved the men and women of the losing tribe as spoils of war. In any case, the people who first bonded them into slavery broke a moral law because they caused harm to those individuals enslaved by taking away their natural freedom. The people who purchased the slaves and later sold them to the slave owner broke a moral law by further promoting the slave business. And the current slave owner who now has to defend his property and moral righteousness promoted the business by purchasing the slaves and abetting the slave trade business. There are many parties to this violation of moral law.

Suppose, however, the soon-to-be slave owner saw the plight of the slaves and, taking pity upon them, decided to try to help them. He purchased the slaves with the idea that in time he could help them regain their freedom and dignity. He used up nearly all of his money to buy the slaves and had determined that once he had recovered his investment, he would set them free. Meanwhile, he planned to provide them with job and language skills as they worked his farm until such time as they repaid him his investment and had obtained the necessary skills to make their way into the world. He envisioned a temporary symbiotic relationship. If the law of the land allows a man to own slaves yet he makes a pact with himself and God to eventually free them, where on the moral scale is the slave owner? Has he simply made a pact with the devil?

Administrative law without the complications of political or ecclesiastical law is necessary to the community if the populace is to be able to go about its business in a productive way. Contrary to universal consensus that lawyers are the spawn of the devil, administrative law begets lawyers, not I. Lawyers become necessary because civil differences of opinion concerning issues of the law or its enforcement are usually administered by a judicial system that requires knowledge of the respective laws of the community. Administrative law covers civil and criminal codes of conduct. It outlines and enforces the rules associated with business and political intercourse within the community.

> *In nature, there are neither rewards nor punishments; there are consequences.*
> —Robert G. Ingersoll

Political Law

In all ages hypocrites, called priests, have put crowns on the heads of thieves, called kings.
—Robert G. Ingersoll

If I exceed the speed limit, I have broken an administrative law. If, as a legislator, I vote for a law that allows for a punitive tax against certain parties that I wish to vex, or passed a law that rewards my supporters at the expense of others, I have created a political law. If I vote for or enforce a law that gives one group an economic or political advantage over another, I have enabled a political law. If I invoke a rule or law that requires a person or group to be persecuted for political reasons, even if I have cloaked the rule or law with the righteousness of moral or administrative law, I have exercised or created a political law. Political law may often use the cloak of patriotism or morality for its origin, but all political laws are ultimately created from a desire to keep or gain influence and power. If I am convicted for sedition or treason, I have violated a political law that is designed to perpetuate the ruling status quo, whether it be benign or malevolent.

A labor union may promote laws that do not allow immigrants to visit the community as workers because the immigrants will work cheaper. Politically, such legislation may protect a particular group within the community, but it may do so at the risk of causing economic damage to others. The employers of the immigrants use them to keep their labor costs low and in some cases keep prices for their products competitive. In this case, a political law that does not permit cheap immigrant labor to be used will benefit the union competing for those jobs, but will push up prices to the consumer. As economic conditions change and if there are too many low paying jobs that union members don't want, the union may lose interest in protecting those jobs, allowing political laws to be passed that promote immigrant labor for certain jobs.

The political process is always in transition, and political laws change with cultural and economic conditions. Politicians in a republic or democracy often pass laws that have nothing to do with moral law or administrative law. Many political laws are passed to further favor with the politician's constituency. They may pass an ecclesiastical law under the guise of moral legislation, or they may pass a political law and call it an administrative law, but a political law will always favor one group over another or one group's welfare to the detriment of the whole. Political laws are often hard to recognize, but if one has the time to track down the true origin of a political law, invariably there will be one party that stands to benefit at the expense of others.

In a dictatorship or authoritarian government, political laws tend to be used to camouflage the ruling elite's self-serving purposes or to tighten its grip on the government. Such laws are used to purge any political opposition and often provide special economic privileges to the governing group's family and friends. Political laws in an authoritarian government are rarely confused with administrative law.

Historically, when the Roman Catholic Church dominated the medieval landscape, political laws were synonymous with ecclesiastical laws. This symbiosis occurs when there is no strong separation of church and state. In the Western Hemisphere, common law evolved into administrative law. In the days of King Henry's England, ecclesiastical law and political law clashed when the papacy refused to permit the dissolution of the first of Henry VIII's six marriages so that he might remarry and spawn an heir to his thrown. As the medieval papacy vied with kings and princes over power and lands, ecclesiastical and political laws were often closely tied or irretrievably broken, depending on the politics of the day.

Political law, unlike administrative or moral law, is generally used for purposes of power and hegemony. It is spawned from the least desirable reasons for a law to exist and stems from the more base motives of men. Like ecclesiastical law, it is frequently abused if there are no restraints placed upon it.

Beware the tyranny of the minority.
—Latin proverb

Ecclesiastical Law

*And of all the plagues with which mankind are
cursed, ecclesiastic tyranny's the worst.*
—Daniel Defoe

Ecclesiastical law is law that is sanctioned by religious
authority. By its nature it requires belief in a supreme being.
To the true believer, ecclesiastical law supersedes all other rules
and authorities because it represents God's word and law.
These laws of faith and conduct are generally interpreted and
communicated to the community by a priesthood, group of
clerics, or self-proclaimed prophet. Some philosophers have
confused ecclesiastical law with moral law. Ecclesiastical law
may speak to us through our experiences and our conscience,
but both our experience and conscience are formed to a large
degree by our religious beliefs, which reflect the moral teachings
in our community at the time. Moral law, on the other hand, is
absolute, universal, and not subject to interpretive differences.

A "holy war" might justify terrible acts upon a populace.
A man may kill innocent people, acting out his faith to fulfill
an ecclesiastic command. This individual may be innocent of
violating an ecclesiastical law by virtue of his faith. Nevertheless,
the killing of innocents for any reason is against moral law and
cannot be justified. The ecclesiastical law may say that there are

no "innocents" or that infidels may be slain without prejudice, but this theology is based on some cleric or priest's interpretation of a scripture or command that may be taken out of context or misunderstood. Or it may simply be an immoral theology. In any case, it was written down by a human being who is subject to misinterpretation, bias, error, and possible redaction of his work over time. One reason ecclesiastical law is not an absolute is because it requires interpretation by men, and mankind has proven itself quite capable of fallacious philosophical reasoning throughout history.

Historically, ecclesiastical law has been guilty of the most terrible acts upon the populace. It is guilty of burning victims alive on a stake of heresy during the Inquisition. Papal edicts have condemned entire cities to the sword. Jews stoned to death those who violated Jewish laws or blasphemed.

The death of Christ as related by the New Testament was supposedly called for by the high priest, Caiaphas, for violating the ecclesiastical law against blasphemy. The New Testament would then blame ecclesiastical law at the hands of the Jews for Christ's death. Blasphemy, however, was a Jewish crime to be punished by death from stoning; Christ was crucified. Upon skipping a few legal formalities, Caiaphas handed Jesus over to Roman authority, sharing with Pilate details of the temple incident and warning Pilate of Jesus's (unsubstantiated) claim to be the king of the Jews. Pilate then quickly tried him for the crime of treason and sedition and ordered him crucified according to Roman civil law. Due to the nature of Christ's death by crucifixion, it was a mixture of Roman political law (treason and sedition) under the guise of administrative law (keeping law and order). Ironically, ecclesiastical law was not the direct cause of Jesus's death, in spite of Pilate's supposed appeasement of the temple authorities.

The Mosaic Code of Law, the Torah, was a civil authority for the people of Israel, and Exodus 21–23 is a sampler that many of the Judeo-Christian background rely upon as moral authority for some of their more suspect acts, such as slavery, witch burning, sacrifice of one's firstborn child, and other peculiar beliefs. The Torah outlines Jewish administrative laws. The Ten Commandments are a part of the Torah, being listed in both Exodus 20 and in Exodus 34. Regardless of which of the two biblical versions of the Ten Commandments you prefer to accept, they mix both ecclesiastical law with moral law, as does Mosaic law. Deuteronomy adds to Mosaic law and specifies that the king must be chosen by Yahweh, presumably through a prophet or the priesthood. It also prohibits pagan religions and covers other ecclesiastical rules of conduct.

When ecclesiastical law becomes one and the same as administrative and political law, a theocracy is formed and religious morality as determined by church doctrine becomes the law of the land. Early colonial Massachusetts law in America was an intolerant theocracy, allowing for the fining, beating, and imprisonment of any Baptist or Quakers who set foot on the colony. Countries that consider themselves fundamentalist Muslim states rule by theocracy and tend to be intolerant of other religions or secular rule. Unlike the tolerance practiced by the Muslims prior to the Crusades, more recent Muslim rule by fundamentalists is authoritarian and theocratic. Political, administrative, moral, and ecclesiastical laws are all one under the fabric of Muslim life according to the fundamentalist view. The clerics and imams make and interpret the laws and scripture and would argue that there is no difference between moral law and ecclesiastical law.

Ecclesiastical law represents the law that is based on the doctrine of a religion that dominates a community. In a theocratic state, ecclesiastical law is the law of the land.

Where it is a duty to worship the sun, it is pretty sure to be a crime to examine the laws of heat.
—Voltaire

Summary

Law is not law, if it violates the principles of eternal justice.

—Lydia Maria Child

Administrative law is the workhorse of all societies, helping the populace of a community to function as it goes about its business. Administrative law should be morally neutral, but it is susceptible to corruption from political and ecclesiastic law. Political law knows no loyalties other than those needed to grasp and maintain power and position. It occasionally finds its way into administrative and ecclesiastical law but can also be useful in checking the power of ecclesiastical law intruding upon the community. Ecclesiastic law rests in the holy books of the major religions and invariably creeps into the political and administrative laws of most nations, even those professing to be governed by secular law. It should not be confused with moral law, which is not a creation of man but like natural laws of the universe, exists to be discovered by those spiritually advanced enough to recognize it for what it is. Moral law is absolute and constant on a cosmic level, subject to no interpretation by those who would truly recognize it. Moral law transcends all laws made by men.

The laws created by men are blends of administrative, political, and ecclesiastical legislation. Unto themselves, they are neither good nor evil. Laws are, however, tools that can be used for good or evil. Laws may be well intentioned but produce results that are not good for the community. The law of unintended consequences frequently puts a nasty twist on the plans of men. An enterprising person can use a law to aid himself in the torture or destruction of whatever victim he may wish harm to. The law itself isn't evil but the person using the law as a tool of grief and pain may be considered evil.

Good men must not obey the laws too well.
—Ralph Waldo Emerson

Moral Man vs. Religious Man

I often ask myself uneasily: is religion indeed a blessing to mankind? Religion, which is meant to save us from our sins, how many sins are committed in thy name?
—Raden adjeng Kartini

A religious man is considered a man of God. A religious man is one who has a belief in a higher power and expresses his beliefs through his words and actions. A religious man is a man who tries to live by his beliefs and theology. If you are known as a religious person, people know you as a person who has strong convictions in your faith. You obey ecclesiastical law, and you are at peace with your god and your religion. You are a good person.

In contrast to a religious man, a moral man may not believe in a higher power. A moral person may be a religious person but most likely is, at best, a deist. A moral man lives by a creed he believes is right and just, but he does not consider himself bound by ecclesiastical law. A moral person is one who tries to obtain the level of morality that is represented by the concept of moral law. In essence, a moral man is a spiritual man living outside the confines of the ecclesiastical universe.

A religious man may be a fanatic or zealot in his beliefs. Such a person is willing to impose his beliefs on those in his community and may be willing to kill, in some instances, if he thinks he is justified in God's eyes. The moral man is sometimes willing to share his beliefs with those who wish to learn his values in life, but he does not proselyte his beliefs and values. He lets his actions and conduct speak for him.

The two concepts are often confused and used synonymously when they should not be. A religious person views his righteous cause to the exclusion of most other religions and doctrines. A moral person follows his principles but gives consideration to how his actions affect others. A moral person might be willing to compromise on an issue of major importance to benefit the greater good; a religious person, bound by his theology, cannot.

The religious person is concerned with saving his soul. Doing the "right thing" morally when that inevitable test of character occurs in one's life is not necessarily a religious necessity. If the "right thing" conflicts with theological doctrine, the religious person is absolved from any wrongdoing by his ecclesiastical authorities. If the "right thing" to do is contrary to doctrine, the religious person must obey ecclesiastical law if he wishes to save his soul from perdition. The religious man does not question the morality of his actions if he believes such actions are cloaked in the sanctity of his religion. And if he does question his actions, he will rationalize his acts as necessary for the greater good. It is God's will, and the end justifies the means.

The moral person, when confronted with the same conflict, will do what is morally correct, even if it goes against the wishes of the majority of the community. While the moral man is not hampered by any religious conflict, he must still confront the fact that often one must take an unpopular course to do the "right thing." The moral person does what he thinks is the correct moral choice, but he does so because it is the right thing to do, not because he fears the wrath of God and wants to save his soul. The motives of the religious man are to save his soul and reap the rewards of Heaven. The moral man is motivated by an inner sense of right and wrong. His actions are governed by a selfless desire to conduct himself honorably among the affairs of men. He is guided by his own conscience and not by the institutions of religion.

This is not to say that a religious man cannot be a moral man or that a moral man cannot be religious. But the two concepts are not synonymous and often are in conflict with each other. A moral person will follow his conscience and try to conduct his life honorably within his own conscience, his family, and his community. The religious person will live his life according to the dictates of his religious belief, resisting the many temptations made available to him and trying to conduct himself with piety toward his god.

I maintain that the moral man is superior to the religious man, because the religious man is bound and often blinded by his doctrine. The religious man will act first according to ecclesiastical law before giving consideration to acting on his own conscience. On the other hand, the moral man has a set of standards he attempts to live by which may even be similar to those of the religious man, yet the moral man is never conflicted by ecclesiastical laws and acts on his own definition of what is morally right. He may waiver in his conduct, but the moral man knows what is "right," whereas the religious man can smother his conscience with his religion and rationalize an action that would ordinarily be condemned by the moral man.

A moral man will give his word, and his word is his bond. He can only be released from his pledge by consent of the person to whom the pledge was made. A religious man may give his word as his bond, but that pledge is subject to be amended or broken by virtue of his commitment to a higher authority, that is, his god or his church. Or, like some of the characters in the Old Testament, he may simply hide behind scripture as an excuse to avoid his obligation. A moral man must ultimately be judged by his deeds and actions; a religious man is judged on the strength of his beliefs. Who is the superior man—the moral man or the religious man? With which would you wish to contract your affairs?

Unfortunately, Hell is populated more with religious men than moral men. This may be due to the fact that religious men are constantly condemning each other to Hell because of divergent theologies. True believers are especially vulnerable to damnation curses. Hell was designed for religious people by religious people. It's a little known secret that while anyone can condemn someone to Hell, the recipient of that curse cannot be affected unless he believes in eternal damnation. (This is one of my rules that the church doesn't know about. Belief in God and Christ require a belief in Hell. I make up the rules here.) Moral people (unless they are more religious than moral) exist outside ecclesiastical rule and are not subject to the punishments found within the hierarchy of Hell. Moral men aren't concerned with the souls of their fellow men and thus do not engage in the nasty business of condemning souls to Hell.

Another reason I have more religious men down here is because there are so many religious fanatics who commit atrocities in the name of God. Their priests or clerics may bless their abominable deeds, but God is the final judge of their actions and He apparently takes a dim view of people using His name to justify breaking moral law. (Just like the Jews, I have a covenant with God. He uses me as His hangman.)

Beware the religious man, for his noble deeds are frequently cloaked in motives of personal salvation and he usually lives a sanctimonious life. The moral man's deeds of virtue are done because it is the moral and correct thing to do, and he lives his life in quiet compliance to his conscience. The religious man is my quarry; the moral man is outside my purview.

> *Convictions are more dangerous foes of truth than lies.*
>
> —Friedrich Wilhelm Nietzsche

Sin

*All men are tempted. There is no man that lives
that can't be broken down, provided it is the right
temptation, put in the right spot.*
—Henry Ward Beecher

Sin can be defined as transgressions against divine law as set forth by ecclesiastical authority. Divine law depends upon which divinity one worships. Jews, Muslims, and Christians all profess to worship the same god, yet their laws and rules of conduct vary immensely. So one can sin as a Muslim yet remain chaste as a Jew or Christian. Or one can sin as a Christian, yet remain righteous in the eyes of God as a Muslim or Jew. Sin varies according to religious dogma and the culture of the community. Evil is not normally an attraction for most men, but sin in its various forms has considerable appeal. I do not traffic in evil, but I must admit that I often toy with the consciences of faithful men by tempting them with sins of their religions.

A sinful act is not the same as an evil act. An act of sin represents a transgression against the doctrines of the religion one has adopted. According to Christians, a person can go to Hell for not believing in Jesus Christ, yet lack of faith in Christ is not in itself an evil act. Nonbelief in Christian theology is considered a mortal sin by the church, but for Muslims, Jews,

Hindus, Buddhists, Taoist, Sikhs, pagans, and other religions, this is not a sin. Sin, then, is dependent on how it is defined by the theology that recognizes it.

The three warrior religions tell their true believers that if they sin, their souls are destined for Hell. Their hold on the faithful, especially the Christian and Muslims, depends upon instilling the fear of God and loss of their immortal souls upon the faithful. They even suggest that man is born into this world with the burden of the sins of Adam. Some theologians say all men and women are born as sinners. Does this mean all men and women are inherently evil? Some early Christian church fathers certainly insist that because of a concept they call original sin, man is evil. This means that the day a person is born his soul belongs to Satan; only by embracing God through the belief of the one true religion can that soul be saved.

Of course, there are several ways a devout believer can wash away his sins and avoid the elevator to Hell. These methods of forgiveness depend upon which religion one follows, of course, but the net effect is the same. All theologies offer the means to avoid damnation of the soul and receive the reward of eternal bliss. If you accept and believe the theology, however, you are bound to its rules. If you are answerable to its rules, you must accept its punishments as well as its rewards.

Religious institutions create framework within their theologies of reward and punishment. By this technique, they develop a psychological hold over their members that cannot easily be broken. A person who is brought up from birth believing and practicing the doctrine of any institution that uses reward and punishment as the basis of its existence cannot and will not lightly alter his or her belief. Any thought or position that attempts to challenge that belief will be vehemently contested by both rational as well as irrational means.

The true believer has fallen victim to institutionalized consciousness that passes for divine knowledge. Occasionally, incremental exposure to knowledge and evidence will allow the conditioned mind of the true believer to begin to doubt the dogma learned over a lifetime and open the mind enough to at least allow independent thought. Generally, however, there is no epiphany of doubt. The principle of reward and punishment is as psychologically powerful as the emotions of love and hate. Both concepts represent the bedrock of religious institutions and are entwined into the theologies of men.

By instilling unquestioning faith and belief in their theologies, these religions have created a psychological marker on the minds of their faithful. Born in sin, the faithful are thrown into religious bondage at birth. This psychic debt to God is created by certain organized religions and is secured by the souls of the faithful. To redeem one's soul from this theologically imposed indenture requires redemption by whatever means one's religion dictates. A person must agree to the terms of his faith to save his soul. If he does not, the rules of the game say his soul goes to Hell (or its equivalent).

Organized religion creates the framework of its theology based on reward and punishment, sets forth the rules of the game, and then holds hostage the souls of living men whose minds are locked and chained by their own faith. The clincher to this scam is that both punishment and reward exists only after death. Except for those manufactured by the religion to perpetuate itself, there are no returning witnesses to validate the existence of the promised punishments or rewards. It's a rigged game.

The warrior religions promise their true believers that if they follow the rules and believe, their faith will save them from Hell. Actually, if we examine their dogma closely, we discover that sins can easily be forgiven, and they claim to have the authority to issue their faithful a passport to Heaven—so long as one believes and obeys. But if you do not have faith and if you do not believe, or if you challenge their authority, for this sin they'll condemn you to Hell. The causes are noble and wonderful to the believer. Expressions of love and goodness abound in all religions. But however you wish to express it, the real rules of the warrior religions are cloaked with the warning: believe and be saved, regardless of your sins; but for the sin of not believing, you cannot be forgiven and you will be punished.

Sin is a concept invented by religion to instill moral values into the religious community as well as to secure ecclesiastical compliance from the faithful. The doctrines of most religions offer absolution of sin and salvation of the soul as a reason to belong to the denomination.

I maintain that absolution of sin by any means approved by the church of one's choice will, indeed, cleanse one of sins against that church and its doctrine. However, such absolution cannot provide forgiveness to anyone for sins against God or another living being. No church has the authority to forgive anyone of such transgressions; that right is reserved for God and for those who have been sinned against. No church or its representative can grant forgiveness to anyone for an evil act. That also is God's prerogative and is not within the domain of mortal man. Religions judge and forgive men's sins; God judges the evil that men do. He doesn't delegate that responsibility. Men who think they have saved their souls from Hell by obtaining absolution or forgiveness from their religious clerics or priests have a special place in Hell. Holy water and baptismal dampness turn to steam and evaporate pretty quickly down here.

Sin represents the ecclesiastical equivalent of disobedience. The so-called fall of Adam was due to disobedience. Adam was cast out of Eden, and God's punishment was that Adam was burdened with a lifetime of toil and struggle. Cain murdered Abel and was punished by a promise of protection from God and sent away to the land of Nod where he spawned children and lived happily ever after. As demonstrated in the book of Genesis, disobedience to God is apparently a greater crime than murder.

Organized religion, each denomination assuming the role of God's representative on Earth, continues to put disobedience at the top of the list of sins. They will forgive all acts, all sins against man, no matter how heinous, save the sin of apostasy or heresy. Man has bestowed upon himself the power to forgive sins in God's name so long as they are sins against humanity. Sins against one's religion are more serious and generate an immediate one-way ticket to Hell, compliments of those in charge of soul damnation. The heretic or apostate is anathema to religions. Sinners are forgiven; apostates and heretics are damned. There is certainly no intercession for those damned by their own religions. Most of the inhabitants of Hell were sent here as the result of the sin of disobedience. Proverbially speaking, Hell is full of independent thinkers, humanists, renegades from the church, heretics, and apostates. I don't get many murderers, rapists, thieves, and other dregs of humanity down here, because they all get "saved" by their respective religions. Ah, the zeal with which religions fulfill their holy missions!

> *There is no sin. There are only stages of development.*
>
> —Tibetan proverb

No One Speaks for God

No man does anything from a single motive.
—Samuel Taylor Coleridge

A ny man can safely make the claim that he speaks to God. A simple prayer accomplishes that act. But the man who claims that God speaks to him or that he speaks for God has confused the voice of his own personal god with that of a universal God. Over the centuries, many have claimed to hear the voice of God and so many others have claimed to be working His will. Is it logical to believe that the voice of God heard by God's own chosen prophets could be so inconsistent, leading to so many different beliefs and interpretations of the Bible, the Book of Mormon, the Koran, and others?

The voice of God is not confined to those self-professed individuals who claim to hear God's word and then spread that "Word" to those who have not yet heard it. Man is by any measure, theological or scientific, an imperfect being who is continuing to evolve. God would not choose to use a human vessel as the means to convey a message that He considers important enough that all mankind should know His thoughts or commands. God's options to communicate with humanity are endless. Why would He choose to use one (or a few, over time) human being(s) as his instrument when there are so many better ways to communicate with humanity?

Anything that passes through the mind of man is subject to corruption. Even the most logical scientific theorem is subject to the shackles of its inventor. Einstein, noted for his work with quantum physics, couldn't always agree with the startling conclusions his mathematical equations were leading him to. His religious beliefs (mind viruses), placed at an early age in his mind, gave him pause and forced him to utter the lines, "God does not play dice with the universe." He meant that the apparent randomness and chaos of his science must either be incorrect or that there was something else he was missing in his search for a unified theory of relativity. His religious programming overrode his intellect and made him doubt what his scientific mind was telling him.

All men's minds are already imbedded with mind viruses, or memes. Memes, as they are called in some circles, are not genetically wired but rather represent ideas placed in the minds of each individual since the day of birth. They may be rational and accurate, or they may be the stuff of pseudoscience. Content is irrelevant. These memes are programmed to replicate themselves without regard to truth, logic, or rationality. Any biases or predispositions that are harbored in a person's mind will corrupt that mind and replicate among other minds if communicated to by the host mind. Reprogramming or deleting such memes is extremely difficult. Religious beliefs are strong memes that are fiercely defended by those who harbor them and spread them. Memes are not limited to religious beliefs, of course. There are many other viruses of the mind, such as marketing slogans, political convictions, dogma, music, etc. Our minds are constantly being programmed by books, newspapers, radio and television programming, songs, teachers, parents, and a host of other media.

The mind of a human is like a sponge that absorbs programmable information and ideas from all media. Man tends to rely on intuitive thinking rather than rational thinking, so associative thought dominates his cognitive powers and often leads him to erroneous conclusions that are not totally rational. Man has well documented problems with memory, problems with rational thought processes, and often has problems with overall mental health. Depression, paranoia, schizophrenia, compulsive disorders, and a host of other psychological disorders find their way into the mental processes of man. Often these illnesses are very subtle and unnoticeable by the casual observer, so the pervasiveness of these disorders is difficult to measure.

My purpose here is not to inform or debate how mental viruses are created and spread or debate man's rationality, but rather it is to demonstrate that a man's mind is not a proper vessel for something as holy as the Word of God. The mind of every human being is filled with viruses of thought that are programmed only to replicate themselves at every opportunity, regardless of the validity or usefulness of the meme or the damage it does to the host. Mental viruses survive by replicating; religions grow by spreading the "Word." Is the self-proclaimed prophet simply spreading a meme or is he truly echoing the "Word of God" as given to him by God Almighty Himself?

An omnipotent God could simply place His "Word" into the minds of all men. (A cosmic meme?) He could do so at birth or at some time that a person is receptive to better understand the message. An omnipotent God should have no need to be coy about what He expects His creations to do. Maybe we have been doing what God has intended of us since the creation of Homo sapiens. Perhaps if we simply looked around at the wonders of our world, we might see His message hidden there among the minor miracles of nature. Or perhaps there really is no message other than for us to live, procreate, and die.

Now, of course, we come to the place in our debate when the true believer simply says that it is not for us to know God's will and why He works in His mysterious ways. We must simply have faith in God and trust in His word, whatever that "word" may be or however interpreted. When cornered with inconsistencies or untruths in the Koran or the Bible, the bibliotist will fall back to the argument that this part of the bible is simply an allegory. Or, if that does not work, he will cloak himself in piety and state that one must have faith in the Bible (or Koran) since it is the Word of God (Allah). His final defense is claiming "we cannot know God's will." This we hear from our priests, ministers, clerics, rabbis, and theologians who read it in a holy book of questionable origin that quotes the words of a prophet who claims to speak the word of God.

I must challenge the circular argument that when confronted with tragedy or unfathomable evil, we must simply accept that "we cannot know God's will." If we cannot know God's will, how can those who profess to know and preach the word of God know that what they preach is really God's word? How can the true believer "know" what God wants for us and "know" that his religion is holy, yet tell us that we cannot know God's will when the question and debate reaches the point where the full circle of argument has been completed without validation of God's existence? We *know* what God expects of us but we cannot *know* God's will? What God expects of us *is* God's will—that same "God's will" that we cannot know when the true believer is forced to shrug his shoulders at the unanswerable question directed to him (unless the cleric can come up with a creative interpretation of the scriptures). I suppose we only know what God wants us to know, and He gives us that information through His chosen prophets and disciples, whoever they may be.

Those who say they preach the Word of God must first reconcile their interpretation of what they claim is the gospel with the "Word" as interpreted by hundreds of contradicting faiths. Which religion holds the valid claim to speak for God? God's Word is reputed to be timeless and constant. If the pope speaks for God, why does his voice often disagree with his predecessors and the voices of other theologians, even contradicting them? If Joseph Smith received the word of God from an angel and wrote it down as the Book of Mormon, why does it not compare favorably with the suras of the Koran as received by the Prophet Mohammed? Why are there different versions of the Holy Bible if the Bible is infallible and represents the Word of God? Who really speaks for God?

These questions are rhetorical. Most readers have their own answers to the questions posed in this essay. To those who already have the answers, I challenge you to examine your mind for the replicating viruses that cloud your reasoning before you smugly dismiss this essay as an unsupported challenge to your faith. The questions posed herein can be easily answered, but the premise one must adopt to satisfactorily answer all the questions is anathema to the true believer.

If you have read this far and are still contemplating the answers, consider this: if you closely examine the motives of any person who professes to speak for God, you will find that his primary mission is to spread a doctrine; his secondary mission is to reap a more temporal reward from his efforts, whether it be power, wealth, or fame.

Sincere men can hear voices in their heads, but no one can prove that the voice being heard is the Voice of God. Perhaps it is Satan that is whispering those exhortations that echo through the mind of the self-proclaimed prophet. A sincere man may insist to his followers that he speaks for God but those followers can only rest their faith on the word of a self-proclaimed prophet who has been preceded by countless others like him. Sincere men and women of all faiths can believe that the doctrine they have been taught since birth is the Word of God as spoken from the prophets of God. That belief doesn't make it so.

God can exist without the worship and affirmations of man. Man can know God's word without an interpreter or intercessory. To think that God must somehow need a human voice to communicate with humanity or to interpret His word is to diminish the concept of an omnipotent God. Questioning or doubting those who claim to speak for God does not mean that the skeptic does or does not believe in God. It simply means that the skeptic questions the authenticity of the mortal who claims to be cosmically connected.

One can doubt the messenger and his message without doubting the existence of God. A deist would have no reason to even become involved with this debate, because he doesn't believe that God gets involved with the affairs of men. A theist, however, believes in an active God involved with supernatural revelation. The theist still doesn't have to believe every prophet or oracle that professes to speak for God. The theist might elect to receive supernatural revelation directly from the source without benefit of a prophet's manifesto. Of course, if the theist then decides he should share his personal revelation with others, he becomes a mortal who claims to carry God's word to the world. Thus a new meme of theology is created and begins to replicate itself. God's word, like the universe, continues to mutate and expand.

A fanatic is a man who does what he thinks the Lord would do if He knew the facts of the case.
—Finley Peter Dunne

Man's Need for God

We cannot know reality; we can only perceive it.
—Zog

If there were no God, life would still have meaning to man. The wind would still blow through tall stately trees covering the countryside. Birds would still nest in those trees and sing their songs to the world. Below, ants would move about the earth gathering food and cleaning up after sloppy campers. Babies would still be born to all creatures, predators would still stalk and kill their prey, and the tides would still roll in and out upon the beaches and reefs of the world. The sun would still rise in the east and set in the west and planets of the solar system would continue their orbits around the sun. Life as we know it on Earth would continue—Spinoza loses, Nietzsche and Sartre win.

How do I know this? I can't prove it, because I can't prove that there is or is not a God. But to simplify this argument, I submit that if the absence of God means that the universe ceases to function, none of us—whether citizens of Earth, Heaven, or Hell—would exist to ponder the matter. Under this debatable hypothesis, *God* must *exist if we exist.*

Conversely, one could argue that God does not exist, yet the universe and all its inhabitants still go about their business. There is at least the prospect that God does not exist. Based on this premise, if He does not exist, it must follow that His absence has no bearing on us since we do exist. Thus *God* may *not exist, but we exist.*

All this circular reasoning takes us nowhere, except that it sets forth a framework to get past the theist's argument that we don't know whether or not life would have meaning or even that we would exist without God's presence. The theist will argue that we cannot prove we would exist without God and therefore, at the very least, man *may* need God to exist. (Follow me closely on this, because you know how crafty the Devil can be when he wants to confuse.)

We earlier supported the unproven statement *God must exist if we exist.* We also supported the converse, stating that *God may not exist, but we exist.* Either argument allows us to conclude that whether or not God exists, you and I exist. If we all agree on that statement, we can then establish that for the purposes of this essay, it does not matter and cannot be proved whether God does or does not exist; in either case, life on Earth still exists. To argue otherwise would mean that we would not exist to debate the matter. I'm not here to debate the atheist's point of view that *God does not exist, yet we exist.* We can't prove that God exists or does not exist, but this debate is for the theists and deists of the world. Being of a supernatural nature myself, I am by definition a theist. The argument against the existence of God has merit, but obviously I cannot be the one to address the issue with any credibility. I am God's creature. If I exist, He exists.

So either we operate under the practical assumption that *we exist whether or not God exists,* or we cannot argue the issue at all, since neither we nor God would exist under the alternative hypothesis. Since we're here (or at least we think we exist in this space–time continuum), let's move on.

God does not give life meaning. Man finds meaning in his life from those around him and events that affect his life. He finds meaning in the relationships he forms during his life. He finds meaning in his business or profession, his social affiliations, his religion, his family, and an assortment of unrelated interests outside of family and business. He has a multitude of reasons to find meaning in his life, yet *God could be absent from all of them.* If God did not exist, man's institutions and social fabric would not notice His absence. Man's religions would continue to express faith in God as they perceive Him. Sermons, prayers, and religious ceremonies would continue to be conducted by men of faith. Since the laws of chance and coincidence remain in good working order, prayers would continue to be answered with the same frequency as they are today. Nothing would be different, so long as men of faith believed that there was a God.

Now, quite possibly, if men of faith *knew* that God did not exist, the social fabric that makes up a large part of the world population would be vastly different. There would be no churches, synagogues, mosques, temples, or other holy places of worship as we know them today. Today's monotheistic religions would have to be radically different if they existed at all. There would, however, be places of worship quite different from those we know today, because man is psychologically wired to maintain belief in a supernatural force. If that force is not God, then it may be the forces of nature transformed into a pantheon of gods, it may be a belief in spirits from other dimensions or from other planes of existence, or it may be some type of theology that we have not yet devised during the several millennia of human existence on Earth.

Man's need to believe in God or gods would be supplanted by some other psychologically satisfying panacea. Even if men knew that there is no omnipotent God to whom they can pray and gain comfort from, man's nature being what it is, men would find a substitute for this phenomena and continue to be born, live, breed, and die. Man may crave the psychological dependency of a supernatural power, but that power need not exist for man to find meaning in life and continue to evolve spiritually. Man's fulfillment and happiness in life comes from his *belief* in his gods as opposed to their actual existence. The placebo effect allows belief to act as a psychic balm for the true believer, even if God does not exist.

God, by Christian, Muslim, and most other monotheist definitions, is a perfect entity. Therefore, I submit He has not created a world that is codependent on His existence. God's creations are perfect for the purpose they were created to serve; thus, the universe and our world are perfect. A creation that is codependent upon its creator implies that the creation is not sustainable without assistance from its creator. I do not think a perfect God would create such a flawed and imperfect world.

Those religions that promise Heaven to the faithful imply that the temporal world is imperfect. I say that any imperfections of this world are merely the perceptions of an ungrateful humanity and not the reality of God's creation. A religion that does not seek to appreciate the world as God created it and attempts to create a promissory world does not hold God's creation in very high regard. What ingratitude of God's creature, man, to be so unhappy with His world that he tries to create a better world though myth and illusion! If there were any imperfection of God's creation, it would not be the apparent universal chaos, gratuitous evil, the randomness of death and destruction on Earth, or the cycle of life and death for all creatures; nay, it would be the inhabitation and domination of Earth by man.

After your death you will be what you were before your birth.
—Arthur Schopenhauer

The Philosophers of Mankind

(Western World Edition)

Philosophy: A route of many roads leading from nowhere to nothing.
—Ambrose Bierce

My disappeared friend Ambrose was a bit too harsh in his criticism of philosophy. Philosophy, when reading the actual texts of what the philosophers of the ages have written, may appear to be rather incomprehensible and obscure, but if one takes the time to capsulize the various philosophies, there are some interesting positions. I'd like to take a brief moment of your reading time to introduce you to some of my favorites and some of those with whom I find must have been the models for Ambrose Bierce's cynicism.

Rather than list these minds in some manner of chronological order, I shall divide them into two groups whereby they share certain opinions and stand on common ground, even if they do not necessarily support each other in their total philosophical works.

For reasons that will soon become obvious, my favorite philosophers include Friedrich (God is dead) Nietzsche, Jean-Paul Sarte, David Hume, and—a man after my own heart—Voltaire (Francois-Marie Arouet). I will then pit these cynics, skeptics, and pragmatists against the faith and belief of the opposing group of philosophers.

On the opposing side I offer you Aurelius Augustinus (a.k.a. St. Augustine, Bishop of Hippo), St. Thomas Aquinas, Immanuel Kant, and Soren Kierkegaard. This group represents a strong bias toward *belief* in things that cannot be substantiated or proven. They are apologists and defenders of the faith for true believers.

I am not interested in the complete philosophies of either group. I only wish to demonstrate how diametrically opposed the greatest minds of mankind can be when the subject of religious doctrine and unquestioning faith is involved. The age old battle between faith and reason continues to haunt us.

St. Augustine was a Christian philosopher who believed in faith and surrender of one's self to God and relentlessly attacked heresy within the church. He believed that Christ provided the "light of knowledge" to the human mind. Augustine was one of the first to come up with the idea that an all-perfect God could not create evil, so it follows that things we think are evil must really be unrecognized goodness that would be obvious if we could see the total picture. As a Christian, belief and faith in the Pauline doctrine of Jesus Christ's divinity was the foundation of Augustine's teachings.

St. Thomas Aquinas was another Christian philosopher and scholar who attempted to prove God's existence and that regardless of whether or not one experienced any earthly felicity during one's lifetime, all would be made right after death transported one's soul to see God. St. Thomas taught that one could know that God exists but cannot know what God is like. Aquinas's idea of evil is a bit more ambiguous than St. Augustine's. Aquinas becomes more subjective by stating that *intent* of the evildoer bears responsibility of whether an act is defined as truly evil. By Aquinas's definition, evil is the lack of the goodness that God created in all things. Aquinas also had unquestioning belief in the divinity of Christ and the doctrine of the Catholic Church.

Soren Kierkegaard was a Danish philosopher who maintained that while we cannot prove God's existence, we must offer ourselves to God through a leap of faith. Knowing and understanding our purpose is not necessary; we must live and act with purpose, and we will find meaning in life through a one-on-one relationship with God. Kierkegaard doesn't really stake out a position on evil.

Immanuel Kant believed that reason would eventually bring about a purely rational religion. We know only that which we have experienced. Kant embraces the idea of the soul's immortality even though it cannot be proven. Kant is quoted as stating in his essay: *Critique of Practical Reason*, "I have had to limit reason to make room for faith." Kant's position on evil is that if an act is based on moral law with good intentions, it cannot be evil, regardless of the consequences.

The common thread of these philosophers is that they use logic and reason in their arguments to attack their opponents, *yet they are willing to suspend their reasoning and yield to a "leap of faith" or simply "believe" when matters of the spirit are involved.* Their arguments or definitions concerning the concept of evil are weak and dogmatic.

David Hume was a British philosopher who taught that morality does not require a religious foundation. He was a skeptic and argued fiercely against philosophical proof of God's existence. Hume came up with the concept that our minds organize our experiences, and so objective knowledge cannot exist. Man's belief in God comes not from reason, but from a desire to be happy. God may exist, but we cannot prove it and we should remain skeptical.

Friedrich Nietzsche was a German philosopher who is famous for his pronouncement that God is dead. He taught that no truths are absolute and bluntly condemned many of the religious and philosophical ideas of his day. Nietzsche taught that the universe cares nothing for man or his values. Man's "will to power" drives his universe, and only the strong survive. Nietzsche maintains that there is no God beyond the concepts of good and evil.

Douglas L. Laubach

That is to say, these concepts are reflections of man's reality but there is no God to judge the merits of either. If man is to perfect himself and evolve into a superior "overman," he must do so on his own through his will to power.

Sartre preaches existentialism, which is a term for the concept that life and death are meaningless and it is up to each individual to establish meaning in his or her life. The end of consciousness is the end of meaning. Sartre is a blatant atheist and argued that evil cannot be redeemed and each individual man is responsible for the evil in the world.

Voltaire is more of a cynic than philosopher. But woven into his writings is a thread of antiestablishment and disdain for organized religion. Voltaire did not believe that man is born evil nor did he entertain any of Christianity's doctrines of evil and salvation. His writings are critical of biblical "facts," and he pointedly takes issue with many inaccuracies and passages that are contrary to historical facts relating to the matter. Voltaire is probably the most interesting of this philosophical pantheon to read because he exercises wit and reason in easy to understand, nonacademic prose. (A man after my own heart, I held a special place in Hell for Voltaire, but alas, his passport to eternity bore the name Francois-Marie Arouet. Rumor has it he ended up in Valhalla or perhaps Olympus. In any case, he didn't make the roster for Heaven or Hell.)

My point in this little exercise is to illustrate that while men pretend to logically and rationally debate the philosophical meaning of life and matters of the soul, their differences in opinion are polar. How can educated, highly intelligent men use the same personal observations, have access to the same sources of information, and yet arrive at contradictory conclusions? How can the same men read a book like the Bible and develop major theological differences of opinion and schools of thought?

Competing schools of thought exist only when the subject cannot be conclusively quantified or proven to be factual. Where there are competing schools of thought, there exist opinions and subjective reasoning but no definitive answers. There are no differing schools of thought concerning mathematics, basic physics, or chemistry. These disciplines represent processes of reasoning that are supported by basic theorems and proofs that provide answers that can be verified and duplicated. There is no doubt in the soundness of these disciplines, so there is no need for competing schools of thought.

There are controversial, conflicting, and competing views concerning religion, philosophy, economics, and similar subjects because these subjects cannot be objectively measured nor can any one school of thought be proven more valid than the other. These subjects represent intellectual masturbation and conjecture without any way to conclusively determine their legitimacy. Practitioners of these disciplines who would have people believe that they are better educated, well informed, and have deduced their way through the tangle of choices to arrive at the only reasonable conclusion are deceiving themselves and their followers.

A significant difference between the two groups we just reviewed is that one school of thought was willing to accept certain premises on faith, whereas the other required a more disciplined approach to their philosophical conclusions. One group *assumed* the existence of God whereas the other was either agnostic or atheistic. All had interesting postulates, yet the two groups are diametrically opposed in their positions of reliance on faith.

Perhaps the only thing this proves is that Ambrose Bierce was correct in his surmise, after all.

> *Religion: A daughter of Hope and Fear, explaining to Ignorance the nature of the Unknowable.*
> —Ambrose Bierce, *The Devil's Dictionary*

The Organization

An organization is the weapon of choice for any ambitious man seeking to destroy his enemy in a civilized society.

—Zog

Man creates organizations to sustain his survival and improve his quality of life. Homo sapiens' ability to organize is its greatest strength. It also presents the greatest danger to the individuals that make up that genus. This talent has made man supreme over all other animals. This ability also forces man to develop a response mechanism that requires that he subordinate his individual will to the dictates of the organization of which he is a member. As man creates more complex and sophisticated organizations, his individual freedom is increasingly subordinated to the greater needs of the organization. Gradually, over time, organizational man will come to accept this condition as the natural order of his species. Free will and independent thought then become primitive vestiges of the preorganizational man.

Organizations, like organisms, live, die, reproduce or expand, and—most importantly—evolve. With each evolutionary stage, the organization becomes more dominant over the human thought process. Individual intellect and willpower imperceptibly give way to the "hive mind." Each generation of Homo sapiens becomes increasingly dependent on the structure, systems, and doctrine of the dominant organization at the cost of individual freedom and thought.

As man's society becomes more and more specialized, he becomes extremely dependent upon the organization to act as a broker and facilitator for the various services that are available and necessary in a highly industrialized society. As men become dependent upon each other for the specialized production of goods and services, they must affiliate with those political and economic organizations that provide infrastructure and political power if they are to ensure equal participation in the system for themselves.

The tendency of organizations to coalesce into "the system" is what makes them even more dangerous. "The system" becomes that ambiguous, all-powerful entity that represents the world of the organizational man. During one epoch, the system was known as the tribal period, where hunters and gatherers lived a migratory life ruled by tribal fiat. During another epoch, the system was the combination of church and monarchy creating a hegemony known as the feudal system. Today the organizational man living in highly advanced nations might identify the system as corporate globalism. In some religious theocracies, the system is the institution of religion as practiced in that theocracy. Whatever identity the system takes, it includes the dominant organization of the member as well as several of the subordinate organizations.

Individual liberty and freedom of action become restricted due to the rules set forth by the organizations formed to make the chosen system work. Primitive man had a very similar but much less complicated choice: join the tribe (or clan) or go it alone. Unless you were a Jeremiah Johnson, mountain man extraordinaire, or an Ayla from the Clan of the Cave Bear, you would likely stay with the tribe for protection and other social benefits. Be aware, however, that tribal social security often consisted of sending its old and infirmed out alone into the cold winter night to freeze to death. Sometimes the benefits of the organization are overrated.

Ants, bees, and similar species of insects are well organized. But the individual elements that make up these hives can't exist without being a part of the colony; they are specialized and highly interdependent upon each other for their existence. Divorce from the colony is not an option to its inhabitants. And if the queen dies, the colony dies. Man, on the other hand, can exist independently of a group. He can dissociate himself from the group and still survive as an independent unit. He may not fare as well as if he had the protection of a group, but he can think independently, act independently, and feed himself without dependence on other humans. He is designed to survive outside the group, if necessary. (I have to admit that the hive trait alone is not all that separates man from bug. There are many biological dissimilarities. But there are similarities, also, depending on which genus within the insect order one analyzes. For example, roaches, like humans, live in clusters of close proximity but can often be found as solitary souls in the night. I can see quite a few other similarities between the two species. We have roaches in Hell, too.)

The hive mind does not totally dominate Homo sapiens like it does certain species within the insect world. This independence separates mammalian organization from insect organization. A colony of insects is composed of thousands of separate and specialized creatures each highly dependent on one another for their existence. The hive or colony acts as one sentient entity, whereas the characteristic of a pack or a herd is that of a disparate membership of like species that may or may not remain together, depending upon the protection and benefits gained from being a part of the group.

All human beings, even those avowing total independence of body and mind, are affiliated with at least one organization at most times in their lives. The basic dominant organizational unit is the family, which can and often is superseded by a more influential organization as the individual expands his or her social base. Some organizational ties exhibit no influence at all on the individual; others can mean the difference between life and death to the individual. In some societies, the family unit (clan) or a religious organization may be the dominant organization; in others, the government dominates. Whatever the culture, every person finds himself affiliated with an organization of some type. And that organization, no matter what it professes to its members, requires a certain level of subordination of the individual's will. *It is the nature of the organization to require individual subordination of free will.* The extent of independent free will sacrificed by its individual members depends on the nature of the organization and the discipline it demands from its membership.

Most humans are affiliated with more than one organization, but all persons are affiliated with at least one, even if it is an involuntary association. An individual may be affiliated with several organizations at several levels. These organizations can range from social to economic to political to religious. There may be minor organizations within the dominant organization, as well as associations outside the universe of the dominant organization. For example, a person can belong to a church and to a church group within that church, as well as to a political party, a fraternal organization, and a business organization. That same person lives under the laws of an organized government.

The self-stated goals of each of these organizations may or may not be separate and of a distinct nature from each other. One organization will always be the dominating entity that influences how that person will interact with the subordinate organizations in his life. There is always a dominant organization influencing the life of the individual, whether it is a voluntary association (such as a social or business affiliation) or a self-imposing organization (such as family, a government, or the mafia). The dominant organization may differ at various stages in one's life, but a dominant affiliation will always exist.

The individual may feel more loyalty to a subordinate organization, but because of the nature of the dominant organization, that individual will succumb to the will of the dominant organization to the detriment of all other affiliations and even his own well-being. The degree of influence the dominant organization maintains over the individual depends on the degree of control exercised over its members by that organization as well as the will and intellect of the individual. The classic battle between the might of the organization and the will of the individual is the stuff of legends.

Organization has allowed man to battle his way out of primeval chaos to rule all other creatures on the planet. Organization is the key to man's evolution and survival. Alas, it may be his future. Man's intellect has allowed him to create more sophisticated organizations than the prehistoric clans that were the forerunners of today's organizational efforts. The institutions he has built are the results of man's ability to organize into diverse groups of individuals seeking common cause. But before we explore those institutions any further, let's first define what it is we seek to examine. What are the traits of an organization, and how do the organizations created by men differ?

Voice or no voice, the people can always be brought to the bidding of the leaders.
—Hermann Goering

Types of Organizations

Public morals are natural complements of all laws: they are by themselves an entire code.
—Napoleon Bonaparte

For the purposes of this essay, an organization can be defined as one or more groups or cells, each comprised of three or more people all working for a common cause. There are four basic types of organizations, which could be divided into many subgroups should one wish to further delineate the characteristics of each. For our purpose, we'll focus on the broader, more basic groups and concern ourselves with the features that set these primary groups apart from each other.

- **Spontaneous organizations** (mobs, anarchic gatherings, political demonstrations)
- **Affiliations** (loosely connected associations, fraternal organizations)
- **Natural organizations** (family, tribal, clans, herds)
- **Structured organizations** (military, business organizations, cults)

The Nature of Organizations

The nature of organizations can be for business purposes, religious purposes, civic purposes, social purposes, political purposes, military purposes, or just about any purpose put forth by man. Organizations are a tool that men create to reach a common goal. Unfortunately, the tool frequently develops an agenda outside its creator's original mission. (Some might say that the hierarchy of Hell was a creation of God that developed its own agenda. Legend has it that God's original purpose was to create a place for the punishment of mankind. I'm not certain what the common goal of Hell is for all us demons, but getting out is probably the common goal of any tortured human souls inhabiting Hell.)

Once an organization reaches a certain size, it takes on a life of its own; the will of its creators and the individual will of its members become subordinate to the will of the organization and the few who control it. The organization's nature to perpetuate itself eventually dominates the purposes for its creation, because it can outlive its creators or because it outgrows them. Once the original creators of an organization are no longer a political or moral force within the organization, the organizational mind becomes the dominant driving force behind the structure. The organization and its controlling group becomes an entity accountable only to itself and whatever sovereign it operates under. Man, as a member of the organization, becomes the servant rather than master of his fate. Man's independent thought and free will become the enemy of the organization. Individual thought that is not within the organization's approved precepts becomes a threat to the organization and is rooted out. Nonconformists are not welcome.

The nature of all successful organizations is to survive, perpetuate themselves, and expand. That is to say, all organizations, if they are to continue to exist, will expend whatever efforts necessary at whatever costs to its members to survive and expand. The original reason for the organization's existence becomes secondary to its survival and perpetuation. Like any living entity, its primal purpose is to survive. It does this through assimilation, evolution, and expansion.

Perpetuation of the organizational entity becomes the primary mission of the organization, superseding the original reason for that organization's existence. Benevolent organizations generally spend more resources on self-perpetuation than they do on their original humanitarian missions. Corporations created for a particular business and driven by economics will quickly purge their ranks of loyal employees, dump or sell affiliates, and, if necessary, go into a completely unrelated business to perpetuate themselves. To survive, they will merge or be assimilated by a larger organization. Fraternal organizations often lose sight of their original reasons for existence but will continue to solicit new members so that the club can avoid extinction. Churches continue to proselytize and compete for new members while often exhorting unlimited procreation upon their members so that as an organization they can expand. They proclaim to seek to save individuals' souls, but the primary benefits of additional membership are economic and political advantages to the organization, not the individual. Soul saving is a secondary mission for organized religion.

The Controlling Elite

Man typically allows his dominant organizations to become his master rather than the instrument of his success. He allows a privileged few to gain control of the organization and exercise dominion over his individual liberty. For the majority of associates in an organization, individual gain is usually only an inadvertent by-product of membership. Only the few, the elite core within each organization, stand to enjoy purposely designed benefits as the result of their affiliation with the organization. These individuals are the controlling authority within the organization who exercise political and economic control. The majority of the membership is used to support the privileges of a small faction who exercise control over the organization. The individuals who make up the controlling group act as the brain of the organization. Just as the organization's nature is to expand and perpetuate itself, their nature is to perpetuate their control of the organization.

The controlling authority does not necessarily contribute to the vibrancy and power of an organization. The controlling elite only directs the majority and enforces the organizational culture. *The power of an organization must come through the degree of commitment of its membership.* A highly motivated membership leverages the effectiveness of an organization *so long as that membership is allowed to exercise its independent will.* The strengths and effectiveness of an organization depends not on its size, but rather it is geometrically proportionate to the discipline and sense of purpose of its members. Once that commitment and discipline is gone, the organization becomes stagnant, bureaucratic, and ceases to expand.

A small but committed group can vanquish a much larger opposing force that has little or no resolve to take up the fight. Such groups or cells can actually subvert a larger organization and seize control, becoming the new controlling authority. This may be done either covertly or by direct confrontation. The organization then begins to evolve and transform itself into an organization with a purpose neither its creators nor their successors originally intended. It is metamorphosed by its new controlling authority. The organization survives; its original purpose has probably changed or been supplanted, and the remaining membership will either support the evolved entity or, if they have a choice, will seek out another organization that better matches their interests.

Organizations exercise varying degrees of control over their members. A dominant organization can display characteristics ranging from a loose affiliation of individuals to a stage of anarchy to a tightly controlled authoritarian entity that controls all aspects of its members' lives.

The natural organizations, such as a tribal or family affiliation, require some acquiescence by the younger members to the elders and perhaps a loss of some autonomy by the individual members due to assumed responsibilities required by the affiliation. But these natural organizations have proven over time to be primarily benevolent. Spontaneous organizations, such as anarchy, may be violent and severe, but they are temporary conditions and are quickly replaced by any one of several competing types of organizations. Loose affiliations are generally democratic and allow the individuals to exercise free will and independence. This independence requires that the organization appear benevolent if it is to win the hearts and souls of its members and perpetuate itself. By definition, a loose affiliation with an organization implies voluntary membership, and that membership is contingent upon an inviting climate.

It is the structured organization that typically provides most of man's misery. These can become closed organizations without escape and require subserviency of independent will by the membership. When the membership allows its will to be dominated by a small, elite controlling group, it allows that group to leverage itself into absolute power. This power cannot later be recalled by a repentant membership.

When an organization is allowed to establish authoritarian control over its members, the degree of commitment of its individual members may be severely diminished, but the power vested to the controlling authority compensates for lack of commitment on the part of the membership. Individual will is replaced by the will of the controlling elite. At this point, power of the organization comes from the ability of the controlling authority to maintain its dominion over the membership. Commitment of the membership is no longer necessary so long as the membership does not actively oppose the controlling authority. A neutral membership provides a favorable climate for any controlling authority. The organization will not expand except by force, but it can survive indefinitely so long as the membership does not actively oppose it. Any future organizational change generally requires an outside force or an opposing controlling authority from within the organization to effect change.

Now we come to the crux of the matter: It is the organization that enables man's penchant for doing evil in great scale. The efforts of an institution's membership may be usurped by the controlling elite who use those efforts in ways hidden from the membership. A stated mission may be announced for the organization that is benevolent to the world. Yet the top echelon, those at the highest level of the hierarchy, may use the organization's resources for purposes the membership would be appalled to discover.

Examples of such duplicity by organizations during the twentieth century include the German Nazi Party's successful effort to politically subvert the republic and gain control of the political institutions of the country, Bolsheviks in Russia using ignorant peasants to make a violent grab for political supremacy under the cover of a benevolent socialist government, covert actions and assassinations by various governments' agencies to overthrow foreign governments, terrorist organizations using unsuspecting charitable organizations or subverting them to raise and funnel money to finance their terrorist agendas, dozens of corporate organizations created for legitimate business purposes but profiting only the controlling elite who were lining their pockets with bonuses and salaries at the expense of their membership (employees and shareholders), and labor unions professing to be protecting the membership only to be drawing high salaries and funneling money to criminal organizations who were infiltrating them at the top levels of the hierarchy. The list of wrongs perpetrated by organizations could fill volumes.

Of course, the list of individuals who have done evil things to their fellow man could also fill volumes—nay, megabits. (Hell recently had to upgrade its data processing system and add considerable memory just to hold the complete list of people condemned to the lower regions. As one might surmise, Heaven has use of the "cloud"; Hell gets the obsolete stuff.) And yes, many organizations have done much good for mankind. Like anything else discovered or created by man, the organization can be a tool for good as well as for evil. In the proper hands, the organization can be benign, if not benevolent.

However, I submit that the amount of evil and suffering that organizations can impose upon men is enormous and question whether or not man is capable of using a tool as dangerous as the organization. Which men are qualified to wield such a tool? Over the last few thousand years, these institutions have given us an endless succession of wars and devastation, religious persecution, genocide, economic panics, and a host of lesser evils too numerous to list.

I watch in awe as religious, political, and economic organizations use the cover of their stated missions to enrich and perpetuate the power of the elite controlling authorities that inhabit these institutions. These organizations are dominant organizations that control the economic and political lives of their members. They are trusted by their members. These organizations are directed by the watchmen and benefactors of the societies they profess to serve and protect.

My questions remain rhetorical: Do the benefits organizations provide to the progress of mankind outweigh the harm they are capable of doing to the individual and his ability to exercise his free will? Are the flawed institutions of man in their current form worth giving up any of the natural freedoms men traditionally hold sacred? Are the watchmen worthy of the trust their members have granted to them? With apologies to Alan Moore, who watches the watchmen?

> *Through the organization, at a terrible cost to the individual, all things are possible for man.*
>
> —Zog

Observations from Hell

Men can acquire knowledge but not wisdom. Some of the greatest fools ever known were learned men.

—Spanish proverb

I have asked my associates here in Hell to contribute to this work. They each have their own unique observations of mankind and of theology in general. Below are some thoughts that represent a parallax from the fallen angels of Hell.

Man's Conceit

We perceive all that is wrong with God's creation from our simplistic point of view that we are privy to all that God has created. But the reality is that we are simply unable to comprehend the magnitude of this complex, multidimensional universe. It serves our purpose to simplify our perception of the vastness of God's work and our own reason for existence. Thus there are those who say that God created man in His likeness and the world for the benefit of man. I say that man has attempted to create God in his image, giving God the human frailties and inadequacies that man recognizes in himself. Man, in his conceit, has attempted to define his gods based on a very limited ability to truly grasp the concept of an omnipotent creator. By trying to define, worship, and humanize God, man has diminished the magnitude and profoundness of the concept we know as God.

—Lucifer

Philosophy vs. Theology

Philosophy attempts to rationally debate the existence and nature of God based on man's perception of the universe. Theology debates doctrine and attempts to devise tenets for belief, which turn into creeds that are often contradictory and confusing. Theology is religion; philosophy is thought. Don't confuse the two.

—Baal

Theism vs. Deism

By definition I am a theist. A theist is one who believes in God as the creator of the universe who remains active in its affairs through supernatural revelation. If Satan truly exists, he exists as a creation of a god that continues to take an interest in humanity. The concept of Satan is tied to the existence of the warrior religions' concept of God as the ruler of the universe. A deist, by contrast, is one who believes in a god who created the world but who is no longer active in the affairs of his creation and remains indifferent to its fate. Satan would not exist under deism.

—Belial

Holy Instincts

Religion, for all but the most devout men, is simply a primitive survival reflex; like the wild animal that instinctively views any unfamiliar sight or sound as a threat to its existence and reacts to minimize the danger to itself, so does the average man by professing his belief in the god or gods of his society.

—Iblis

God Is Good?

Where is it written (with authority) that God is good? Why does He have to have that characteristic? When men debate the issues of good and evil, the primary assumption is that God, by definition, is "good." Because of that assumption, moralists find themselves defending a theodicy that cannot be intellectually defended. If God is good, why did He create evil and why does he allow it to exist? If He did not create evil and has no sovereignty over evil, then God did not create everything in the universe and is not omnipotent and the theodicy of monotheism crumbles.

The theologian's response is that God did create evil, but when evil occurs, there is a greater good that occurs. This greater good outweighs the apparent pain and destruction caused by the evil act. Unlike an all-knowing God, we simply cannot know the full implications of how an apparently evil act actually does more good than harm. It is much like looking at a penciled dot on a piece of paper. In a two dimensional universe, all we see is the dot. In a three dimensional universe, we can see that a pencil rises from the dot's point on the paper. The theologian argues that we live in something like the two dimensional universe whereas God lives in the three dimensional universe and has insight we can never know.

If, however, we make the assumption that God is neither bad nor good, there is no need to defend his reputation or heap adulation upon him. Evil exists, but it is simply one of the universal laws of God's creation. God created evil on this world because it was necessary. One might ask why it was necessary; the obvious response is that we cannot know the full implications of evil in the world. We live in something like a two dimensional universe …

—Asmodeus

Monotheism

Monotheism is touted by its adherents to be superior to polytheism. Polytheists learned several millennium ago that they had to respect others' gods and be tolerant toward competing gods. Over time, clans and city-states absorbed the gods of their neighbors and expanded the pantheon as needed. Monotheists came along and annihilated any competing beliefs along with the citizens that practiced them. Monotheists are extremely intolerant of competing religions and even root out and exterminate heresies within their own theology. The reason polytheism is nearly extinct today is because the monotheistic warrior religions have eradicated all competing beliefs and have narrowed the field of competition. There are fewer gods to worship and fewer doctrines to choose from. Man will soon suffer from an oligopoly of religious doctrine. The monotheists are now fighting among themselves for supremacy. Most likely Armageddon, if and when it finally arrives, will be between two remaining monotheistic religions each accusing the other of being the forces of evil.

—Satanael

Holy Books

Holy books, such as the Pentateuch, the Tanakh, the Bible, the Koran, the Vedas, and all the other professed "Gospels" of faith, are born of political necessity rather than divine inspiration. They are penned to document and reinforce the theology that created them. To say such books are divinely inspired is an affront to whatever god they purportedly came from. Such ego mocks the intelligence of God, who wouldn't claim authorship of any literature so flawed and error-ridden.

The Old Testament portion of the Christian Bible is the Jewish Tanakh with a few books rearranged. The Catholic version of the Bible has a few extra books that the Protestant version doesn't include, and both of them omit books for their own reasons that were not included in the original assemblage of these tomes (the Apocrypha and pseudepigrapha).

The original books of the Christian Bible were often blatant plagiarisms from Babylonian, Syrian, and other texts of antiquity. For example, the Babylonian god, Enlil, decides to destroy mankind with a flood. The Babylonian equivalent to Noah is told about the plan by another god, Ea. On the seventh day, the rains stopped and the Babylonian Noah's boat stopped on the mountain of Nisir. (Ararat?) Similarly to the Hebrew version, doves and ravens are sent out. Life goes on. The Roman version has Jupiter (Zeus to the Greeks) doing the same, and his "Noah" lands on Mt. Parnassus. The Hindus have their Noah story, also. Moses has parallel myths that preexisted the Jewish version. Mises, Perseus, Osiris, Sargon I, and other pagan mythical beings share very similar histories with Moses.

Without documenting the many other corresponding myths that are shared by both the ancient Hebrew tribes and their influential neighbors, suffice it to say that the Jewish religion, from which Christianity was spawned, is an amalgam of the various gods, cultures, laws, and beliefs of various civilizations of the era. The original authors of the Old Testament even help separate symbolism from facts through the use of Midrashes. Call the stories pagan if you wish, but they are the primeval legends from which the Bible narratives were created. Taken literally, if carefully read, the Bible is filled with contradictions and error. Taken symbolically, the errors can be attributed to translation, misunderstanding, or an assortment of apologetic excuses. They can be mitigated by such works as the Midrashes, or in the case of the Koran, the Hadith. In any case, when one examines its origin, the Bible is best read as symbolic myth rather than literal fact.

The Koran has similar questionable issues and errors of fact. A book dictated to a prophet from an infallible God should be free of grievous error. To briefly illustrate my case, consider the issue of the Satanic Verses, or note how much of the material in the Koran comes from the Pentateuch, or the contradictory use of first person and third person in certain suras when God is supposed to be the sole speaker. Consider that there are apparent missing verses in the Koran as we now receive it, and of course, as in all the holy books, the usual variant versions of the same "Gospel."

The Hindu Vedas are mythological in their scope and highly dependent upon proper translation from the Sanskrit. It's pretty difficult to address any errors or omissions, since the Vedas do not profess to be based on actual historical events on Earth. It's just one massive parable. Vedic knowledge as written in the Gita is the infallible word of Lord Sri Krsna (Supreme Lord). As with any religious philosophy or theistic "science," proof of origin and verification of the supernatural are not within the ability of mortal man living on this earthly plane. The Hindus do a better job of dispensing the "Word of God," because the only controversy is in the accuracy of translation, and if one reads the Vedas, they can be indecipherable whether translated correctly or not. We can question the translations and the Hindu philosophy, but unlike the amalgam of history and myth found in the Bible, the Vedas are pure myth.

These books may have all once been the infallible word of God, but by using man as a vessel to communicate any holy book, it becomes defiled. If such a thing as a holy book could truly exist, why would God not use a more direct approach so that His word could be reported accurately without any distortion or doubt? People who believe in an infallible word of God written down in holy books by biased and flawed mortals are assuming that God is either stupid or unfathomable. (Unfathomable: "God works in mysterious ways.") And since there is more than one claim to infallibility by the competing and irreconcilable holy books, which one is God's true infallible Word?

—*Azazel*

Moloch's View of Heaven and Hell

Everyone knows what Hell is like. They've been told by their priests, rabbis, masters, preachers, and anyone professing to know God and the works He wants done in His name. Conjure up whatever vile, horrible, and demonic vision your mind can create, and that is the Hell to which you will be doomed should you stray from the path of righteousness. Likewise, whatever you think Heaven will be like when you die is the Heaven that awaits you. Why? Because the concepts of Heaven and Hell are creations that were spawned from the minds of mortal men with vivid imaginations and good intentions. (What is it they say about the road to Hell and good intentions?) The vision becomes the promise, and the promise becomes your destiny.

Creations such as Heaven and Hell become reality only through belief. They exist because they were placed in your mind by doctrine and theology. If you truly believe you will go to Heaven when you die, that is your destiny. No church or religious organization can deprive you of that unless you accept their doctrine over your own sense of goodness. Your salvation is within you and is dependent solely upon how strong you believe in an afterlife and the nature of that afterlife. If you believe you are an evil person and have damned yourself to Hell, then plan on it. If you believe you have done whatever is necessary in your mind to gain access to Heaven, then plan on the rewards of Heaven. Death, as in life, has its choices.

Every true believer has his or her own image of Heaven and Hell, and each of these believers has his or her idea of the rite of passage to gain entry into either of these worlds. Their realities may be the same or differ; it matters not in this world and in this life, however, because upon death the natural laws of the universe as they are known to man no longer apply. The spiritual realities during life are viewed from a different perspective after death.

The dirty little secret no one wants people to know is that *everyone* goes to Heaven. All but the mentally deranged or incompetent believe they are worthy for Heaven—even those whom others might judge as evil. Few people truly believe that they, themselves, are evil beings who will go to Hell for their earthly actions or beliefs. If they believe in the cosmology of God and Satan or some similar cosmology, they expect to go to their concept of "Heaven." Others believe in reincarnation so for them, at least during their earthly existence, Heaven and Hell are moot issues. The poor souls we get down here are mostly demented and tortured spirits who were indoctrinated by some religion to the point that they really believed they were Hell-bound. You get what you believe in this universe, my friend.

I do not wish to overly complicate the subject of Heaven and Hell, and Satan has restricted the space I can devote to the subject, so I will save elaboration of this topic for another time and leave the reader with this thought: Once you die, either there will be or will not be an afterlife. If there is no afterlife, it matters not to you, for you no longer exist in body or soul. If there is an afterlife, it will be made of the stuff of your dreams, not the dreams of others, unless you let their dreams become your dream. If you are a true believer and there is an afterlife, your goodness and worthiness coupled with your trust in a just and fair God will fare you well. Judge not others, but be generous in your self-judgment.

—Moloch

God's Design

How benevolent is a God who creates creatures to inhabit a world that, by design, requires them to kill and eat each other to survive? Satan might be accused of such diabolical design but he is absolved because God is given the credit for this piece of work.

—Beelzebub

Fellowship vs. Ceremony

I note with amusement that religions cloak themselves in ceremony and take their rituals very seriously. Men and women must find other places to fraternize and develop relationships, since religions do not sanction playful fellowship among their members. Frolicking and merrymaking may lead to something evil in the eyes of the pious, so such activities are often banned or discouraged by religious clergymen who are concerned that their brethren might become tempted to sin if they are having too much fun.

This serious business of saving souls is a grim task, indeed. I suspect that religious propriety is more important to the ecclesiastics than the fellowship that men crave and enjoy. How somber are the ceremonies and doctrines of many religions! Why must the joy of fellowship among men be subordinated to religious liturgy?

—*Lilith*

The Root of All Evil

Money, it has been said, is the root of all evil. Whoever coined that tiresome cliché didn't fully understand the true nature of man. Yes, the desire for wealth and power has often driven men to do shameful things. Yet if wealth alone were a bad thing, many biblical characters—such as Job, Abraham, Solomon, and others—would not have been blessed by their God, YHWH. Mohammed the Prophet died a wealthy man. Many church organizations are very wealthy. Are these men and institutions tainted by their wealth? Biblically speaking, then, money would be evil unless it is in the possession of the church or one who is blessed by God (or His representatives). Money, for those who aren't willing to use it to further God's purposes, could be called evil.

Money itself is simply a tool to be used like any other instrument. In itself, it is not evil, but like political, legal, or ecclesiastical power, it can be used to foster abuses and evil deeds if the bearer so directs it.

The unrelenting drive to acquire material wealth at the cost of developing one's personal wealth of character is a shameful thing but is not evil. It is a major character flaw, but it is no more evil than obsession toward other things. St. Augustine of Hippo, Buddha, and other men of God deserted their families for personal ecclesiastical pursuit. Were they any less obsessed than the man obsessed with material wealth?

Man is driven to do bad things when he lusts after things he does not have. Things not yet attained but sorely coveted can drive a man to heinous crimes if he suffers from weak character. But wealth and money are only examples of things coveted by men. In the same category we can place women, power, status, political freedom, knowledge, and even the salvation of one's soul. Are these yet to be attained but coveted goals evil unto themselves?

The root of all evil in man is his own selfishness and greed; let's not misplace the blame. The root is fed by the things man wants but cannot acquire, but it is a weak man who allows these things to successfully torment him at the expense of his honor and integrity.

—*Mammon*

Religious Rationalization

Man's ability to rationalize and then call the resulting conclusions logically sound should astound me, but over the ages I have grown weary of his tiresome game. Early Christian church fathers used all kinds of circular logic to justify their positions. Men like Tertullian, Irenaeus, Nestorius, Cyril, Augustine, and others argued such theological issues as the divine nature of Christ, original sin, what constituted heresy, and other esoteric topics. The result of three hundred years of debates, political chicanery, and ecumenical councils was a doctrine for the Catholic Church and the creation of something they now call the Trinity. Obviously, the theology they created wasn't as simple as Christ's original teachings to his Hebrew brethren.

The concept of the Trinity is the result of all the compromise and philosophical debate of the early church fathers. It is the end product of the brilliant minds that developed Christian theology. Since the concept is not logical nor is it monotheism, I find it interesting to listen as theologians try to explain and defend it. First we had God. Then we had Jesus Christ. And then the Holy Spirit (Holy Ghost) was proclaimed a part of the Deity. From here on, the topic becomes buried in opinion and debate. Thus man can rationalize himself out of any philosophical quandary and convince others as to the legitimacy of his conclusion.

I have watched while inquisitors used such logic against old women accused of being witches and have been present when people accused of heresy and witchcraft were burned at the stake because the superstitious fools thought that fire was the only way to destroy the devils within. These same inquisitors believed that Hell is an inferno where Satan and his demons reside. Why then, would earthly fire destroy what Hellfire would not?

I watch as men write down their beliefs in books they call bibles or holy books. Then I watch them dispute the meaning of those same books as the need suits them. Such books they frequently term the "Word of God" are replete with passages that are misinterpreted, fraudulent, translated incorrectly, allegorical, taken out of context, or simply not what the author(s) meant. Rationalization creeps in the back door as credibility slips out the front.

Religion has demonstrated to me that it is intellectually dishonest and incapable of engaging in philosophically meaningful debate. It always ends up requiring that the true believer have "faith" in what he or she is being told. I would hold any creed with great suspicion that builds its foundation on something as tenuous as faith, especially when the storyline is as incredible as that of Christianity. However, having watched the performance of those who exhort their followers to have faith and believe, I can only marvel at how well the masses have been taught to accept the conclusions of such irrational thinking. The same goes on among Muslims, Hindus, Buddhists, and others; Christians just do it best.

—*Mephistopheles*

The Inhabitants of Hell

Hell has some qualities and attractions that might be of interest to those considering that inevitable change of venue at some time in their future. As we all know, life has only one real certainty. After that, it's all speculation and hope, so you should at least be prepared for any detours on your journey to Heaven. Of course, we're all going to go to Heaven, aren't we? However, in the unlikely event that you somehow end up in Hell before you get to Heaven, you may be interested in a piece of trivia about the place.

For those who have a distinct dislike for people of other faiths, you will be pleased to know that for the warrior religions and monotheists, Hell is segregated. Muslims go to Christian Hell, Christians go to Muslim Hell, Jews are sent to Jewish Hell, Christian Hell, or Muslim Hell, depending on the faith of the person condemning them to Hell. Buddhists, Hindus, and Confucians have an entirely different menu from which to choose, but they, too, have designated areas of confinement; they are placed in with the pagans, atheists, and polytheists. No self-respecting monotheist would be caught dead around these kinds of sinners.

—*Abaddon*

Bibliography

(With apologies to those whose works in the genre are of equal value and merit but not listed. Like the universe and the creation, this list is a work in progress and continues to expand.)

*Titles that are recommended reading are marked with an asterisk.

—*Satan*

1. Russell, Jeffrey B. *Lucifer: The Devil in the Middle Ages*. Ithica, NY: Cornell University Press, 1986.

2. Russell, Jeffrey B. *Satan: The Early Christian Tradition*. Ithica, NY: Cornell University Press, 1987.

3. Martin, Malachi. *The Decline and Fall of the Roman Church*. New York, NY: Bantam Books, 1981.

4. Robertson, J. M. *Pagan Christs*. New Hyde Park, NY: University Books, Inc., 1967.

5. Anderson, C. Alan, PhD. *The Problem Is God*. Walpole, NH: Stillpoint Publishing, 1985.

6. Sheehan, Thomas. *The First Coming*. New York, NY: Vintage Books, 1988.

7. Hubbard, L. Ron. *Dianetics*. Los Angeles, CA: Bridge Publications, Inc., 1986

8. Whitehead, Alfred North. *Religion in the Making*. New York, NY: New American Library, 1996

9. *The Lost Books of the Bible, Translated from the Original Tongues*. New York, NY: Bell Publishing Co., 1979

10. Graham, Lloyd M. *Deceptions and Myths of the Bible*. New York, NY: Bell Publishing Co., 1979

11. Lohr, Andrew. *Talks on Mystic Christianity*. Ojai, CA: Fiery Water Press, 1984

12. Williams, Caroline. *Saints: Their Cults and Origins*. New York, NY: St. Martin's Press, 1980

13. Aveling, J. C. H. *The Jesuits*. New York, NY: Dorset Press, 1987

14. *The Book of Jasher*, version by Alcuin. San Jose, CA: Rosicrucian Order, 1971

15. Friedman, Richard Elliott. *Who Wrote the Bible?* New York, NY: Summit Books, 1987

16. Robinson, James M., general editor. *The Nag Hammadi Library*. San Francisco, CA: Harper & Row, 1981

17. Paine, Thomas. **The Age of Reason*. Buffalo, NY: Prometheus Books, 1984

18. Holzer, Hans. *The New Pagans*. Garden City, NY: Doubleday & Co., 1972

19. Kant, Immanuel, and Werner Pluhar. *Critique of Practical Reason*. Indianapolis, IN: Hackett Publishing Co., 2002.

20. Percival, Harold Waldwin. *Thinking and Destiny*. Dallas, TX: The Word Foundation, Inc., 1981

21. Woodrow, Ralph. *Babylon Mystery Religion*. Riverside, CA: Evangelistic Assoc. Inc., 1981

22. Carter, Lee, PhD. **Lucifer's Handbook*. Academic Associates, 1977

23. Edmond Paris. *The Secret History of the Jesuits*. Chino, CA: Chick Publications, 1975

24. **The Urantia Book,** Authors Unknown. Chicago, IL: Urantia Foundation, 1981

25. **Holy Bible, Revised Standard Version**, Authors Unknown. Teaneck, NJ: World Publishing Co., 1962

26. **The Koran,** translated by N. J. Dawood. New York, NY: Penguin Books, 1978

27. **The Book of Mormon**, as "translated" by Joseph Smith Jr. Salt Lake City, UT: The Church of Jesus Christ of Latter-Day Saints, 1985

28. **Bhagavad Gita**, As It Is, Translated by A. C. Bhaktivedanta. Los Angeles, CA: Swami Prabhupada, The Bhaktivedanta Book Trust, 1985

29. Doane, T. W. *Bible Myths and Their Parallels in Other Religions*. Mokelumne Hill, CA: Health Research, 1985

30. Graves, Kersey. *The World's Sixteen Crucified Saviors* (Or, *Christianity Before Christ*). New York, NY: The Truth Seeker Co., 1960

31. Smart & Hecht, Editors. *Sacred Texts of the World*. New York, NY: The Crossroad Publishing Co., 1982

32. **The Torah** (*The Five Books of Moses*). Philadelphia, PA: The Jewish Publication Society of America, 1962

33. Foxe, Rev. John, as edited by Marie Centertking. *Foxe's Book of Martyrs*. New York, NY: Jove Books, 1982

34. Pagels, Elaine. *The Gnostic Gospels*. New York, NY: Vintage Books, 1981.

35. Wells, G. A. *The Historical Evidence for Jesus*. Buffalo, NY: Prometheus Books, 1982

36. Fox, Robin Lane. *Pagans and Christians*. New York, NY: Alfred Knopf, Inc., 1989

37. Barnstone, Willis, editor. *The Other Bible*. New York, NY: Harper & Row, 1984

38. Schonfield, Hugh J. *After the Cross*. La Jolla, Ca: A. S. Barnes & Co., Inc., 1981

39. Burman, Edward. *The Templars: Knights of God*. Rochester, VT: Thorsons Publishers, Inc., 1986

40. Partner, Peter. *The Murdered Magicians*. Rochester, VT: Thorsons Publishers, Inc. 1987

41. Eusebius. *The History of the Church*. New York, NY: Dorset Press, 1965

42. Chadwick, Henry. *The Early Church*. New York, NY: Dorset Press, 1967

43. Chamberlin, E. R. *The Bad Popes*. New York, NY: Dorset Press, 1969

44. Grant, Michael. *Jesus, an Historian's Review of the Gospels*. New York, NY: Charles Scribner's Sons, 1977

45. Nietzsche, Friedrich. *The Anti-Christ*. New York, NY: Penguin Books, 1982

46. Mencken, Henry L. *The Philosophy of Friedrich Nietzsche*. Torrance, CA: Noontide Press, 1982

47. Voltaire. *Philosophical Dictionary*. New York, NY: Penguin Books, 1972

48. Harwood, William. *Mythology's Last Gods*: *Yahweh and Jesus*. Buffalo, NY: Prometheus Books, 1992

49. Romer, John. *Testament*. New York, NY: Henry Holt & Company, 1988

50. Armstrong, Karen. *Muhammad: A Biography of the Prophet*. New York, NY: Harper Collins Publishers, 1992

51. Armstrong, Karen. *A History of God*. New York, NY: Alfred Knopf, 1993

52. Sanders, E. P. *The Historical Figure of Jesus*. Middlesex, England: Penguin Books, 1993

53. Carmichael, Joel. *The Birth of Christianity*. New York, NY: Dorset Press, 1992

54. Burman, Edward. *The Inquisition: Hammer of Heresy*. New York, NY: Dorset Press, 1992

55. Griffiths, Major Arthur. *In Spanish Prisons*. New York, NY: Dorset Press, 1991

56. Christie-Murray, David. *A History of Heresy*. New York, NY: Oxford University Press, 1976

57. Strayer, Joseph R. *The Albigensian Crusades*. Ann Arbor, MI: Ann Arbor Paperbacks, 1992

58. Maccoby, Hyam. **The Mythmaker: Paul and the Invention of Christianity*. New York, NY: Harper Collins, 1986

59. Mack, Burton L. *The Lost Gospel: the Book of Q & Christian Origins*. New York, NY: Harper Collins, 1993

60. Smart, Ninian. *The Long Search*. Boston, MA: Little, Brown and Co., 1977

61. Paine, Lauran. *The Hierarchy of Hell*. New York, NY: Barnes & Noble, 1995

62. Potok, Chaim. **Wanderings*. New York, NY: Fawcett Crest Books, 1978

63. Jones, Terry, and Alan Ereira. *Crusades*. New York, NY: BBC Books/Facts on File, 1995

64. Hoffer, Eric. **The True Believer*. New York, NY: Harper & Row, 1951

65. Payne, Robert. *The History of Islam*. New York, NY: Barnes & Noble, 1992

66. Haught, James A. *Holy Hatred*. Amherst, NY: Prometheus Books, 1995

67. Jockle, Clemens. *Encyclopedia of Saints*. London, England: Alpine Fine Arts Collection, Ltd., 1995

68. Daniell, David. *William Tyndale: A Biography*. London, England: Yale University Press, 1994

69. Redford, Donald. *Egypt, Canaan, and Israel in Ancient Times.* Princeton, NJ: Princeton University Press, 1992

70. Shanks, Hershel. *Understanding the Dead Sea Scrolls.* New York, NY: Random House, 1992

71. Levy, Leonard W. *Blasphemy.* New York, NY: Alfred Knopf, 1993

72. Warraq, Ibn. *Why I Am Not a Muslim.* Amherst, NY: Prometheus Books, 1995

73. Pagels, Elaine. *The Origin of Satan.* New York, NY: Random House, 1995

74. Larson, Charles M. *By His Own Hand upon Papyrus.* Grand Rapids, MI: Institute for Religious Research, 1992

75. Vermes, Geza, Translator. *The Complete Dead Sea Scrolls in English.* New York, NY: Allan Lane, 1997

76. Smith, Huston. *The Religions of Man.* New York, NY: Harper & Row, 1965

77. Gaer, Joseph. *What the Great Religions Believe.* New York, NY: Signet, 1963

78. Dimont, Max. *Jews, God and History.* New York, NY: Signet, 1962

79. *Porphyry's Against the Christians.* Amherst, NY: The Literary Remains, Prometheous Books, 1994

80. *Josephus: The Complete Works,* translated by William Whiston. Nashville, TN: Thomas Nelson Publishers, 1998

81. Stanton, Graham. *Gospel Truth?* Valley Forge, PA: Trinity Press, 1995

82. Davis, Kenneth C. *Don't Know Much about the Bible.* New York, NY: William Morrow & Co., 1998

83. Akenson, Donald. *Surpassing Wonder: The Invention of the Bible and the Talmuds.* New York, NY: Harcourt Brace & Co., 1998

84. Russell, Bertrand, edited by Paul Edwards. *Why I Am Not a Christian and Other Essays*. New York, NY: Simon & Schuster, Inc., 1957

85. Macmullen, Ramsey. *Christianity & Paganism in the Fourth to Eighth Centuries*. London, England: Yale University Press, 1997

86. Mccabe, Joseph. *The Forgery of the Old Testament and Other Essays*. Buffalo, NY: Prometheus Books, 1993

87. Ellerbe, Hellen. *The Dark Side of Christian History*. San Rafael, CA: Morningstar Books, 1995

88. Ingersoll, Robert. *Some Mistakes of Moses*. Amherst, NY: Prometheus Books, 1986

89. Eisenman, Robert. *James the Brother of Jesus*. New York, NY: Viking Press, 1996

90. Asimov, Isaac. *Asimov's Guide to the Bible*. New York, NY: Wings Books, 1969

91. Green, Ruth Hurmence. *The Born Again Skeptic's Guide to the Bible*. Madison, WI: Freedom from Religion Foundation, 1999

92. Halpern, Baruch. *David's Secret Demons*. Grand Rapids, MI: William B. Eerdmans Publishing Co., 2001

93. Mckinsey, C. Dennis. *The Encyclopedia of Biblical Errancy*. Amherst, NY: Prometheus Books, 1995

94. Kugel, James L. *The Bible As It Was*. Cambridge, MA: Harvard University Press, 1997

95. Brust, Steven. *To Reign in Hell*. New York, NY: Tom Doherty Associates, 1984

96. Bernstein, Alan E. *The Formation of Hell*. Ithaca, NY: Cornell University Press, 1993

97. Bamberger, Bernard J. *Fallen Angels*. New York, NY: Barnes & Noble Books, 1995

98. Ludemann, Gerd. *Heretics, the Other Side of Early Christianity.* Louisville, KY: Westminister John Knox Press, 1996

99. Ingersoll, R. G. *Complete Lectures of Col. R. G. Ingersoll.* Kila, MT: Kessinger Publishing, LLC, 1900

100. Persuitte, David. **Joseph Smith and the Origins of the Book of Mormon.* Jefferson, NC: Mcfarland & Co. Inc., 1985

101. Brodie, Fawn M. **No Man Knows My History.* New York, NY: Vintage Books, 1995

102. Roberts, R. Phillip. *Mormonism Unmasked.* Nashville, TN: Broadman & Holman Publishers, 1998

103. Smith, Joseph, Jr. *Doctrine and Covenants/Pearl of Great Price.* Salt Lake City, UT: Deseret Book Company, 1969

104. Corydon, Bent. *L. Ron Hubbard, Messiah or Madman?* Fort Lee, NJ: Barricade Books, Inc., 1992

105. Atack, Jon. *A Piece of Blue Sky: Scientology, Dianetics and L. Ron Hubbard Exposed.* New York, NY: Carol Publishing Group, 1990

106. Sagan, Carl. *The Dragons of Eden.* New York, NY: Random House, 1977

107. *The World Almanac & Book of Facts: 2011.* New York, NY: World Almanac Books, 2011

108. Parrinder, Geoffry. *World Religions.* New York, NY: Facts on File, 1983

109. Greenberg, Gary. *101 Myths of the Bible.* Naperville, IL: Sourcebooks, Inc., 2000

110. Sheehan, Thomas. *The First Coming.* New York, NY: Random House, 1986

111. Wilson, A.N. *Jesus-A Life.* New York, NY: W. W. Norton & Co., 1992